INTRODUCTION: THE POWER OF MOTTAINAI

In this introductory chapter, we delve into the fascinating concept of Mottainai and its significance in today's world. Derived from Japanese culture, Mottainai urges individuals to cultivate a deep sense of regret over waste and embraces the idea of 'no waste' in all aspects of life.

At its core, Mottainai encapsulates the belief that resources should not be squandered but instead valued and utilized to their fullest potential. This concept resonates strongly in our current environmental landscape, where issues such as climate change, overconsumption, and resource depletion loom large.

By embracing Mottainai, we can make a meaningful contribution towards a sustainable future. It encourages us to adopt mindful consumption practices, reduce waste, and make conscious choices that prioritize longevity and durability. Through these actions, we not only conserve resources but also tap into a profound source of personal and societal transformation.

Mottainai calls upon us to reevaluate our relationship with the material world and shift away from a throwaway culture. It emphasizes the importance of cherishing what we have and using it wisely instead of mindlessly discarding it. By doing so, we can create a ripple effect that extends beyond our own lives and positively impacts communities and the planet.

The significance of embracing Mottainai cannot be overstated.

It offers us an opportunity to reconnect with nature, honor our cultural heritage, promote economic efficiency, and forge deeper connections with one another. As we navigate a time of ecological urgency and widespread calls for sustainable living, Mottainai provides a powerful framework for action.

Throughout this book, we will explore the myriad ways in which Mottainai can be incorporated into our modern lives. From sustainable living practices to cultural preservation, economic efficiency to mindful consumption habits, we will uncover the various facets that make Mottainai a catalyst for global transformation.

Join us on this journey as we unlock the potential for a happier, richer, and more fulfilled life through embracing Mottainai. By the end of this book, you will have the tools and insights to make a positive impact on the world and create a sustainable future for generations to come.

Historical Background of Mottainai:

To truly understand the power and significance of Mottainai, it is essential to delve into its rich historical background rooted in Japanese culture. The concept of Mottainai has deep-seated ties to traditional practices, craftsmanship, and resource utilization that have been ingrained in Japanese life for centuries.

In ancient Japan, the scarcity of resources and the need for frugality shaped the mindset of the people. Mottainai emerged as a response to this reality, emphasizing the importance of making the most out of what one possesses. It was a way of life that honored and respected resources, ensuring that nothing went to waste.

Throughout Japanese history, Mottainai found expression in various domains. From the exquisite art of repairing broken pottery with gold lacquer, known as kintsugi, to the meticulous use of every part of an animal in traditional cuisine, Mottainai permeated every aspect of daily life. It became a philosophy that not only promoted practicality but also celebrated the beauty and value inherent in every object, regardless of its perceived usefulness.

Mottainai was closely intertwined with Japan's cultural heritage, as it aligned with principles of simplicity, mindfulness, and gratitude. It guided artisans in their creations, who carefully selected materials and diligently crafted items that could withstand the test of time. It fostered a deep appreciation for the natural world and its resources, shaping traditional practices like Ikebana (flower arrangement) and tea ceremonies.

As time progressed and Japan experienced periods of rapid modernization and industrialization, the concept of Mottainai faced challenges. The rise of mass production and consumerism introduced a culture of disposability that contradicted the principles of Mottainai. However, there has also been a resurgence of interest in Mottainai in recent years as people recognize its relevance in addressing contemporary environmental issues.

Understanding the historical roots of Mottainai allows us to appreciate its enduring wisdom and relevance in our modern lives. It provides a foundation for embracing Mottainai as more than just a cultural artifact but as a dynamic force that can guide us towards a happier, richer, and more fulfilled existence. By learning from the past, we gain valuable insights on how we can incorporate Mottainai into our present-day practices and contribute to a sustainable future.

The Impact of Mottainai:

Embracing Mottainai has the potential to create a profound impact on individuals, communities, and the world as a whole. By adopting the principles of Mottainai, we can lead happier, richer, and more fulfilled lives while also contributing to the greater good.

One of the key impacts of Mottainai lies in promoting mindful consumption. In a society driven by excessive consumerism and wasteful practices, embracing Mottainai encourages us to pause and reflect on our consumption habits. By cultivating a deep sense of regret over waste and practicing 'no waste' in all aspects of life, we become more conscious of the resources we use and the impact they have on the environment. This shift towards mindful consumption not only reduces waste but also helps preserve natural resources for future generations.

Moreover, Mottainai fosters sustainable living practices. From reducing single-use plastics to supporting local and sustainable businesses, embracing Mottainai inspires us to make choices that align with environmental conservation. By consciously choosing eco-friendly alternatives and incorporating sustainable habits into our daily routines, we contribute to a healthier and more resilient planet.

In addition to environmental benefits, embracing Mottainai can also lead to economic efficiency. By prioritizing quality over quantity and making informed purchasing decisions, we can save money in the long run. Investing in durable products that are built to last not only reduces the need for frequent replacements but also supports businesses that prioritize sustainability. This shift towards economic efficiency not only benefits our personal finances but also contributes to a more sustainable economy.

Furthermore, adopting Mottainai principles can have a ripple effect within communities. When individuals come together to embrace Mottainai, they create a collective impact through shared values and practices. Communities that value resource utilization, minimalism, and mindful consumption can collaborate on initiatives such as community gardens, sharing libraries, or swapping events. These initiatives not only foster a sense of belonging and mutual support but also create opportunities for collaboration, learning, and positive change.

Illustrating the impact of Mottainai are numerous examples and case studies from around the world. From individuals leading minimalist lifestyles to organizations implementing innovative waste reduction strategies, the positive outcomes of embracing Mottainai principles are evident. These real-world examples serve as sources of inspiration and motivation for readers to embrace Mottainai in their own lives.

Embracing Mottainai has the power to transform our personal lives, our communities, and ultimately, our world. By mindfully consuming resources, promoting sustainability, and cultivating a deep appreciation for what we possess, we can create a future that is happier, richer, more fulfilled, and in harmony with the environment.

Overview of the Book's Purpose and Structure:
This book serves as a comprehensive guide for individuals seeking to embrace the transformative power of Mottainai in their lives. It is designed to provide both inspiration and practical strategies for adopting Mottainai principles, ultimately leading to personal and global transformation.

Structured into fifteen chapters, each section explores a different aspect of Mottainai and its applications. By delving into its historical roots, examining its connection to sustainable living, economic efficiency, cultural preservation, and more, this book offers a holistic understanding of Mottainai's potential impact.

The purpose of this book is twofold: to inspire readers to adopt Mottainai as a guiding philosophy and to provide actionable steps towards incorporating it into daily life. It aims to empower readers with the knowledge and tools needed to make positive changes in resource utilization, consumption habits, and community engagement.

Each chapter contributes to this broader exploration by highlighting specific aspects of Mottainai and offering practical tips, case studies, and thought-provoking anecdotes. By following the progression of chapters, readers can gradually deepen their understanding of Mottainai and its potential for personal and societal transformation.

Throughout the book, readers will also find illustrations, visuals, and exercises that enhance their learning experience and encourage active engagement with the material. The intention is to create a compelling narrative that inspires readers while providing them with tangible strategies for incorporating Mottainai principles into their own lives.

By the end of this book, readers will not only have a clear understanding of Mottainai but also be equipped with the knowledge and tools necessary to embrace it fully. They will have gained insights into its historical significance, discovered how it aligns with various aspects of modern life, and recognized its potential for creating a happier, richer, and more fulfilled future.

With each page turned, readers are invited on a journey towards embracing Mottainai as a powerful tool for personal and global transformation. The structure of the book aims to guide them through this journey, ensuring that they come away with a deep appreciation for the principles of Mottainai and a roadmap for implementing them in their own lives and communities.

Invitation to Embrace Mottainai:

Now that we have explored the concept of Mottainai and its historical roots, it is time to invite you, dear reader, to embark on a journey towards embracing Mottainai principles. As you delve into the pages of this book, I encourage you to approach it with an open mind and a willingness to make positive changes in your life.

Embracing Mottainai is not just about adopting sustainable practices or reducing waste; it is about embracing a mindset that values every resource and sees the potential for transformation in what others may discard. By cultivating a deep sense of regret over waste and seeking ways to maximize the utility of our resources, we can create profound positive change in our own lives and in the world around us.

I believe that each one of us has the power to make a difference. By embracing Mottainai, we can unlock the incredible potential for happiness, richness, and fulfillment that lies within a mindful and appreciative approach to resource consumption. We have the opportunity to shape a future where waste is minimized, sustainability is prioritized, and generations to come will inherit a world that thrives.

Through the chapters ahead, you will be introduced to practical strategies, inspiring case studies, and thought-provoking anecdotes that will guide you towards adopting a lifestyle rooted in Mottainai principles. From sustainable living practices to cultural preservation efforts, economic efficiency to mindful consumption habits, you will discover the many facets that make Mottainai a catalyst for personal and global transformation.

I am optimistic about the transformative power of Mottainai. I am confident that as we embrace its principles and infuse them into our daily lives, we will not only experience personal fulfillment but also contribute to a more harmonious relationship between humanity and the planet we call home.

So, let us embark on this journey together. Let us embrace Mottainai and become agents of change, living with intention, appreciation, and respect for the resources that surround us. The power to create a happier, richer, and more fulfilled future lies within our hands. Are you ready to join the movement? Let us begin.

UNDERSTANDING THE ROOTS: EXPLORING THE HISTORY OF MOTTAINAI IN JAPAN

The origins of Mottainai can be traced back to the cultural roots of Japan, where it holds significant meaning. In order to fully understand and embrace the concept of Mottainai, it is essential to delve into its historical background and explore the traditional practices and beliefs that shaped it.

Mottainai finds its roots in the deep reverence that the Japanese people have for nature and the resources it provides. Throughout history, Japan has been a nation that highly values sustainability and resourcefulness. This mindset stems from the belief that wasting any form of resources is not only detrimental to society but also disrespectful to nature itself.

Ancient Japanese practices such as Shintoism and Buddhism have greatly influenced the development of Mottainai. The principles of these religions emphasize harmony with nature, respect for all living things, and an awareness of the interconnectedness of life. These foundations laid the groundwork for Mottainai to become deeply ingrained in Japanese culture.

The concept of Mottainai was further shaped by traditional practices like tea ceremonies, where every element is appreciated, respected, and utilized to its fullest extent. Additionally, the art of Ikebana (flower arrangement) exemplifies the idea of Mottainai by carefully selecting and arranging flowers in a way that honors their beauty and transience.

Throughout Japan's history, resource scarcity and limited land availability played a significant role in shaping Mottainai practices. The Japanese people developed innovative techniques such as mingei (folk crafts) and wabi-sabi (the acceptance of imperfections) to transform and repurpose materials, thereby minimizing waste.

By understanding the cultural roots of Mottainai, we gain valuable insights into the deeper significance of this concept. It serves as a reminder that embracing Mottainai is not just about conserving resources but also about honoring our connection to nature, preserving cultural heritage, and living in harmony with the world around us.

Mottainai throughout Japanese History: Evolution and Adaptation

Throughout the course of Japanese history, Mottainai has stood as a powerful concept, adapting and evolving to meet the changing needs of society and the environment. By exploring key moments in Japan's past, we gain valuable insights into how Mottainai played a pivotal role in resource utilization and conservation.

One notable period where Mottainai took center stage was during the Edo period (1603-1868). This era was characterized by a focus on simplicity, frugality, and mindfulness in daily life. With limited resources available, the people of Japan embraced Mottainai as a way to make the most of what they had. Waste was seen as not only wasteful, but also disrespectful to the resources that were used to create it. This mindset led to a culture of repairing and repurposing items rather than discarding them.

Another significant moment in Japanese history that highlights the importance of Mottainai is the post-World War II era. In the aftermath of destruction and scarcity, the concept of Mottainai became even more essential. With limited resources and a need for economic recovery, the Japanese people mobilized their collective efforts to rebuild and repurpose materials. It was during this time that Japan's reputation for innovative recycling and conservation practices began to take shape.

In more recent years, Japan has faced environmental challenges brought on by rapid industrialization and urbanization. Despite these obstacles, the spirit of Mottainai has endured. The country has implemented policies and initiatives to promote sustainability, including strict waste management systems and a focus on renewable energy sources. These efforts serve as testament to Japan's commitment to embracing Mottainai principles for a more sustainable future.

By examining these historical moments, we see how Mottainai has continually adapted to new circumstances and remained relevant throughout Japanese history. Its significance lies not only in conserving resources but also in fostering a deep respect for the natural world and the materials it provides. These lessons from Japan's Mottainai legacy inspire us to embrace similar practices in our own lives and communities, ultimately leading to a more sustainable and fulfilled existence.

Cultural Significance of Mottainai: A reflection of values and beliefs

Mottainai holds a deep cultural significance in Japan, reflecting core values and beliefs that have influenced various aspects of Japanese society. By analyzing the deeper cultural meanings associated with Mottainai, we can gain a greater understanding of its profound impact on Japanese art, fashion, and architecture.

In Japanese culture, Mottainai represents a sense of regret over waste and an appreciation for the value inherent in all resources. It is rooted in the concept of "mottai," which refers to the intrinsic worth or potential within something. This belief that everything possesses inherent value has shaped the Japanese mindset towards resource utilization and preservation.

One area where the influence of Mottainai is particularly evident is in the realm of art. Traditional Japanese art forms, such as pottery, calligraphy, and ikebana (flower arrangement), emphasize the importance of utilizing materials efficiently and mindfully. Artists strive to bring out the true beauty and potential of each material, embodying the spirit of Mottainai.

Similarly, Japanese fashion has been profoundly shaped by Mottainai values. The concept of "mottainai fashion" promotes the idea of prolonging the lifespan of garments through repairs, alterations, and repurposing. This approach not only reduces waste but also celebrates the unique stories and memories associated with clothing, fostering a greater appreciation for the resources invested in their creation.

Mottainai's influence also extends to Japanese architecture, where principles of sustainability and resourcefulness are deeply ingrained. Traditional houses are designed with a keen awareness of nature's rhythms and resources. The use of natural materials that are locally sourced and easily replenished reflects a deep respect for the environment and a commitment to sustainable living.

By exploring these various aspects of Japanese culture influenced by Mottainai, we gain valuable insights into how this concept can be embraced in our own lives. Beyond conserving resources, Mottainai invites us to cultivate a profound appreciation for the value and potential inherent in everything around us. By embodying these values, we can not only contribute to a more sustainable future but also experience a deeper sense of fulfillment and connection with the world around us.

Mottainai Rituals and Traditions: Preserving heritage through mindful practices

Throughout history, Japan has developed a rich tapestry of rituals and traditions that exemplify the principles of Mottainai. These practices not only honor resources but also promote sustainability and foster a deep connection to nature. In this section, we will explore specific rituals and traditions rooted in Mottainai principles, showcasing their significance in preserving heritage and inspiring mindful practices.

One such practice is the traditional Japanese tea ceremony, known as Chanoyu. This centuries-old ritual centers around the careful preparation and serving of matcha, powdered green tea. The tea ceremony embodies Mottainai by emphasizing the appreciation of every moment and every aspect of the tea-making process. From the selection of utensils to the choreographed movements of the tea master, no detail is overlooked. By valuing each element, participants develop an acute awareness of the resources involved, leading to a deeper connection with the natural world.

Shinto shrines also provide a glimpse into Mottainai principles. Shintoism, Japan's indigenous religion, holds nature in high esteem and encourages a harmonious relationship with the environment. At shrines across Japan, visitors can witness rituals that honor nature and express gratitude for its abundance. For example, during Hatsumode, the first shrine visit of the year, people offer prayers and make offerings to deities associated with natural elements such as water, trees, and mountains. This act of reverence reinforces the idea of considering resources sacred and treating them with utmost respect.

Festivals, or Matsuri, are vibrant celebrations deeply ingrained in Japanese culture. These events often revolve around themes of agricultural harvests, changing seasons, and ancestral traditions.

Matsuri offer an opportunity to showcase Mottainai principles through various activities such as parades, performances, and food offerings. For instance, in the Yamabushi festival held in Nagano Prefecture, participants pay homage to the mountains by engaging in rigorous hiking and performing traditional rituals. By involving the community in these festivities, Mottainai principles are passed down through generations, instilling a sense of responsibility and appreciation for natural resources.

These examples illustrate how Mottainai rituals and traditions permeate various aspects of Japanese life. They serve as reminders of the importance of preserving heritage while embodying mindful practices that align with sustainable living. By participating in these rituals, individuals not only experience a deeper connection to nature but also gain a sense of purpose and responsibility towards resource conservation.

As we explore the rituals and traditions rooted in Mottainai principles, it becomes clear that they have the power to inspire individuals and communities worldwide. By embracing these practices, we can honor our own cultural heritage while working towards a more sustainable future. Let us now reflect on the enduring relevance of Mottainai in contemporary Japanese society and how these historical lessons can guide our path to sustainable living.

Modern-day Relevance: Lessons from Japan's Mottainai Legacy

As we explore the history of Mottainai in Japan, it becomes apparent that its principles and practices continue to hold immense relevance in contemporary society. In a world grappling with environmental challenges and a growing need for sustainable living, we can draw valuable lessons from Japan's Mottainai legacy.

One of the key lessons we can learn from Japan is the importance of mindfulness and appreciation for resources. The concept of

Mottainai encourages individuals to cultivate a deep sense of regret over waste and to make the most out of what they possess. This mindset shift has profound implications for our modern-day concerns surrounding resource conservation and responsible consumption.

In today's fast-paced consumer culture, where disposable products dominate the market, embracing the Mottainai philosophy can offer a much-needed alternative. By adopting a more mindful approach to resource utilization, we reduce waste and extend the lifespan of our belongings. This shift not only benefits the environment but also helps us reconnect with the value inherent in our possessions.

Japan's Mottainai legacy also teaches us about the power of community and collective action. Throughout history, Japanese communities have come together to implement Mottainai practices, realizing that sustainable living requires cooperation and shared responsibility. This spirit of collective effort can inspire individuals and communities worldwide to work towards a more sustainable future.

Furthermore, Japan's Mottainai legacy demonstrates the potential for creativity and innovation in resource utilization. Traditional Japanese art forms such as kintsugi (repairing broken pottery with gold) and boro (repurposing worn-out textiles) exemplify the beauty that can emerge from reimagining and repurposing what may be seen as waste. These examples inspire us to think beyond conventional notions of waste and explore creative solutions that are both practical and aesthetically pleasing.

Finally, Japan's enduring commitment to Mottainai serves as a powerful reminder that sustainable living is a continuous journey. The history of Mottainai in Japan shows us that it has evolved and adapted over time to meet changing societal and environmental needs. In our rapidly evolving world, it is crucial to remain open to new approaches and possibilities, always seeking innovative ways to integrate Mottainai principles into our lives.

The lessons learned from Japan's Mottainai legacy are not confined to its borders. They resonate with individuals and communities worldwide who seek a more sustainable way of life. By embracing the enduring relevance of Mottainai, we can cultivate a profound appreciation for resources, foster a sense of collective responsibility, stimulate creative problem-solving, and embark on a journey towards a more sustainable and fulfilling future.

MOTTAINAI AND SUSTAINABLE LIVING: REDUCING WASTE FOR A GREENER FUTURE

Introduction to sustainable living practices

Sustainable living is a fundamental aspect of addressing the pressing environmental challenges we face today. As our planet grapples with issues such as climate change, deforestation, and resource depletion, it has become increasingly clear that our current patterns of consumption and waste generation are simply not sustainable in the long run.

In this chapter, we explore the importance of sustainable living and how it aligns with the principles of Mottainai. Sustainable living encompasses a wide range of practices and behaviors aimed at reducing our ecological footprint, conserving resources, and promoting a greener future for generations to come.

Mottainai, with its emphasis on regret over waste and the idea of 'no waste', provides a powerful framework for approaching sustainable living. By incorporating Mottainai principles into our daily lives, we can cultivate a mindset that recognizes the value inherent in all resources and strives to minimize waste in all its forms.

While Mottainai originated in Japan, its principles are universal and applicable to individuals from all walks of life. By adopting a Mottainai mindset, we can make conscious choices that prioritize sustainability in every aspect of our lives â€" from the products we purchase to the energy we consume.

As we delve deeper into this chapter, we will explore practical strategies and tips for reducing waste in everyday life. We will examine areas such as food, packaging, and energy consumption, providing actionable steps that readers can take to minimize their environmental impact.

Additionally, we will discuss the concept of the circular economy and how it ties into sustainable living. The circular economy promotes a system where resources are used efficiently, products are designed for durability and recyclability, and waste is minimized through recycling and repurposing. By embracing circular economy principles, we can contribute to a more sustainable and regenerative economy.

Finally, we will highlight the role of Mottainai in fostering sustainable living communities. Through community-driven initiatives focused on waste reduction and resource sharing, we can create supportive environments that encourage sustainable behaviors and promote collective action towards a greener future.

By embracing sustainable living practices guided by the principles of Mottainai, we have the power to make a significant positive impact on our environment and create a greener, more sustainable future for all. In the following sections, we will delve deeper into these practices, providing you with the tools and inspiration needed to embark on your sustainable living journey.

The concept of 'no waste' lies at the heart of sustainable living. It is the idea that every resource, whether it be food, materials, or energy, should be utilized fully and efficiently, leaving no room for waste. Embracing this concept requires a fundamental shift in mindset, one that prioritizes mindful consumption and conscious decision-making.

In today's throwaway culture, where convenience and disposability often take precedence, adopting the principle of 'no waste' may seem daunting. However, by understanding the environmental consequences of our actions and recognizing the immense potential for positive change, we can begin to embrace this transformative concept.

To embrace 'no waste,' we must first become aware of the impact our choices have on the environment. This means understanding the lifecycle of products and resources, from their creation to their disposal. By acknowledging the true cost of waste generation, both in terms of environmental degradation and resource depletion, we can start to value every item and material as precious.

A key aspect of embracing 'no waste' is reevaluating our relationship with consumerism. In a world driven by constant consumption and instant gratification, it becomes crucial to ask ourselves whether we truly need all that we consume. By cultivating a sense of mindfulness and intentionality in our purchasing habits, we can reduce unnecessary waste.

Additionally, transitioning towards 'no waste' living requires us to rethink packaging and single-use items. By opting for reusable alternatives and supporting businesses that prioritize sustainable packaging solutions, we can significantly reduce the amount of waste generated. Simple swaps, such as carrying a reusable water bottle or coffee cup, can make a substantial difference in our individual ecological footprint.

Education and awareness play an essential role in fostering a 'no waste' mindset within individuals and communities. By disseminating information about sustainable practices and providing resources for waste reduction, we can empower individuals to make informed decisions that align with the principles of 'no waste.'

The concept of 'no waste' extends beyond individual actions; it is about creating a circular economy that minimizes waste and maximizes resource efficiency. By embracing practices such as recycling, composting, and upcycling, we can contribute to the creation of a more sustainable and regenerative society. Supporting businesses and initiatives that prioritize circular economy principles becomes crucial in driving systemic change.

Ultimately, embracing the concept of 'no waste' requires recognizing that our individual choices have a collective impact. By making intentional decisions and cultivating a deep sense of responsibility for the resources we consume, we can contribute to building a greener future. Embracing 'no waste' is not just an individual endeavor; it is an invitation to join a global movement towards sustainable living and a more harmonious relationship with our planet.

Tips and strategies for reducing waste in everyday life:

1. Mindful grocery shopping: Plan meals ahead of time, make a shopping list, and avoid impulse purchases. Buy only what you need to minimize food waste.

2. Reduce single-use plastics: Use reusable bags, water bottles, and utensils instead of disposable ones. Choose products with minimal packaging or opt for package-free alternatives.

3. Composting: Start a compost bin or contribute to a community composting program. Composting food scraps and yard waste reduces landfill waste and creates nutrient-rich soil.

4. Repurpose and upcycle: Instead of throwing away items, find creative ways to repurpose them. Turn old jars into storage containers, repurpose clothing into new garments, or transform pallets into furniture.

5. Repair instead of replacing: When something breaks or wears

out, consider repairing it instead of buying a new one. This not only reduces waste but also saves money.

6. Energy-efficient practices: Conserve energy by turning off lights when not in use, using energy-efficient appliances, and adjusting thermostats appropriately. Unplug electronics when they are not in use to prevent standby power consumption.

7. Donate and share resources: Instead of discarding items that are still usable, donate them to local charities or participate in community sharing programs. This extends the lifespan of products and reduces waste.

8. Mindful disposal: Properly dispose of hazardous materials like batteries, electronic waste, and chemicals to prevent environmental contamination. Research local recycling programs for items that cannot be recycled through regular channels.

9. DIY cleaning and personal care products: Make your own cleaning agents and personal care products using natural ingredients. This reduces the need for single-use plastic containers and harmful chemicals.

10. Conscious consumerism: Before making a purchase, consider the product's durability, ethical sourcing, and recyclability. Choose quality items that will last longer, reducing the need for replacements.

By implementing these tips and strategies, individuals can significantly reduce waste in their everyday lives. Embracing Mottainai principles encourages a shift towards mindful resource utilization, leading to a greener, more sustainable future.

Embracing circular economy principles is a crucial component of sustainable living and aligns perfectly with the concept of Mottainai. The circular economy aims to minimize waste and maximize resource efficiency by moving away from the traditional linear model of production, consumption, and disposal.

In this section, we delve into the intricacies of the circular economy and explore its relevance to creating a greener future. We provide a comprehensive explanation of how this innovative approach works and why it is essential for sustainable living.

The circular economy seeks to design out waste and pollution, keep products and materials in use for as long as possible, and regenerate natural systems. It emphasizes the importance of reusing and recycling resources to create a closed-loop system that minimizes environmental impact.

To illustrate the practical application of these principles, we showcase various businesses and initiatives that have successfully implemented circular economy practices. From innovative product design and manufacturing processes to collaborative consumption models, these examples demonstrate how embracing circularity can lead to significant environmental benefits.

We discuss businesses that have adopted strategies like remanufacturing, where products are repaired or upgraded to extend their lifespan. This approach not only reduces waste but also minimizes the need for new raw materials and energy-intensive manufacturing processes. We highlight companies that have integrated recycling programs into their operations, enabling them to transform waste into valuable resources.

Additionally, we explore initiatives that encourage sharing and collaboration among individuals and communities, such as tool libraries, car-sharing platforms, and peer-to-peer rental services. These initiatives help optimize resource use by allowing multiple people to benefit from a single item, reducing the overall demand for new products.

By showcasing real-world examples of businesses and initiatives implementing circular economy practices, we inspire readers to think creatively about how they can incorporate these principles into their own lives. We encourage individuals to support businesses that prioritize sustainability and circularity, as well as consider adopting practices like repairing, repurposing, and sharing resources within their communities.

Together, embracing circular economy principles and practicing Mottainai can create a powerful synergy that fosters a greener future. By challenging the throwaway culture and prioritizing resource efficiency, we can significantly reduce waste and contribute to a more sustainable and fulfilling way of life.

The role of Mottainai in fostering sustainable living communities

Communities play a crucial role in promoting sustainable living practices, and incorporating Mottainai principles can significantly contribute to this effort. By embracing the ethos of 'no waste' and encouraging resource sharing, communities can create a more sustainable future for everyone.

One way communities can apply Mottainai principles is through the establishment of community gardens or urban farming initiatives. These projects not only promote local food production but also minimize waste by utilizing organic waste as compost. By growing their own produce, community members reduce their reliance on commercially packaged foods and contribute to a more sustainable and self-sufficient lifestyle.

Another example of Mottainai-inspired community initiatives is the establishment of tool libraries or sharing centers. These spaces allow community members to borrow tools and equipment, reducing the need for individuals to purchase items that may only be used infrequently. This not only reduces waste but also promotes a sense of camaraderie and collaboration within the community.

Community-driven waste reduction programs can also be implemented through organized recycling and upcycling initiatives. Communities can set up collection points for specific materials like paper or plastic, ensuring that these resources are properly recycled rather than ending up in landfills. Additionally, community workshops or skills-sharing programs can teach residents how to repurpose and upcycle materials, turning waste into creative and useful items.

By embracing Mottainai principles at the community level, individuals can work together to find innovative solutions for reducing waste and promoting sustainable living. Through collective action, communities have the power to create lasting change and inspire others to adopt similar practices. As we recognize the interconnectedness of our actions, we can build stronger, more resilient communities that prioritize the well-being of both people and the planet.

Examples of successful community-driven initiatives focused on waste reduction and resource sharing include the Zero Waste Community Project in Seattle, Washington. This project brings together residents, businesses, and local authorities to work towards creating a zero waste community. Through education, collaboration, and innovative waste reduction strategies, the project aims to minimize waste generation and maximize resource recovery.

In Japan, there are numerous examples of communities that have embraced Mottainai principles to foster sustainable living. One such example is the town of Kamikatsu, known for its commitment to zero waste. In Kamikatsu, residents meticulously sort their waste into over 45 different categories for recycling or composting. This level of dedication has earned the town international recognition as a model for sustainable waste management.

By highlighting these inspiring examples and providing practical guidance, we hope to empower individuals and communities to embrace Mottainai principles and foster sustainable living practices. Together, we can create thriving communities that prioritize resource conservation, waste reduction, and a greener future for generations to come.

THE ECONOMIC EFFICIENCY OF MOTTAINAI: SAVING MONEY THROUGH MINDFUL CONSUMPTION

In this chapter, we delve into the economic advantages of embracing Mottainai principles in our daily lives. By adopting a mindful approach to consumption, we not only contribute to a more sustainable future but also save money and avoid unnecessary expenses.

Many individuals may not realize the hidden costs associated with wasteful consumption habits. Constantly purchasing disposable items or products that quickly wear out or become outdated can be a drain on our finances. The concept of Mottainai encourages us to rethink our relationship with material possessions and make more conscious choices.

By embracing Mottainai, we develop a greater awareness of the long-term value and durability of the items we purchase. Instead of succumbing to trends and buying new products frequently, we learn to prioritize quality over quantity. This shift in mindset leads to significant financial savings as we invest in items built to last.

Furthermore, Mottainai encourages us to consider the true cost of our purchases, beyond their initial price tag. By making informed decisions based on factors such as energy efficiency, resource consumption, and environmental impact, we can save money in the long run. For example, opting for energy-efficient appliances or reducing water usage not only benefits the environment but also reduces utility bills.

Throughout this chapter, we will explore strategies for mindful consumption that enable us to make better financial decisions. We will discuss techniques for evaluating the true value and utility of a product before purchasing it. By asking ourselves whether an item is truly necessary or if there are alternative options available, we can avoid impulsive buying and unnecessary expenses.

Additionally, we will highlight budget-friendly alternatives to wasteful products and practices. From DIY projects to second-hand shopping, there are numerous ways to reduce costs while still fulfilling our needs. We will examine examples of individuals who have successfully embraced Mottainai principles and saved money by repurposing and upcycling existing possessions.

Lastly, we will explore the role of the sharing economy in promoting economic efficiency. Through platforms such as car-sharing or tool libraries, communities can optimize resource utilization and reduce individual expenses. We will showcase successful examples of sharing resources within communities and discuss how these initiatives align with Mottainai principles.

By understanding the economic benefits of Mottainai, we can make informed choices that not only support our financial well-being but also contribute to a more sustainable world. Through mindful consumption, we can save money, reduce waste, and pave the way towards a happier, richer, and more fulfilled life.

Strategies for Mindful Consumption

In our quest to embrace Mottainai and achieve economic efficiency, it is crucial to develop strategies for mindful consumption. By making conscious purchasing decisions and considering the long-term value and durability of products, we can not only save money but also contribute to a more sustainable and fulfilling lifestyle.

One of the most effective strategies for mindful consumption is to thoroughly research and evaluate products before making a purchase. This involves looking beyond price tags and considering factors such as quality, durability, and environmental impact. By investing in products that are built to last, we can avoid the need for frequent replacements and ultimately save money in the long run.

Another important aspect of mindful consumption is avoiding impulsive buying habits. It is easy to be lured by the allure of sales and discounts, but by taking a moment to reflect on whether we truly need an item, we can avoid unnecessary expenses. By practicing restraint and aligning our purchases with our actual needs, we can prevent wasteful spending and prioritize meaningful investments.

Additionally, it is essential to consider the environmental impact of our consumption choices. Choosing products that are sustainably produced, energy-efficient, or made from recycled materials not only reduces our ecological footprint but also often leads to cost savings over time. For example, opting for energy-efficient appliances or LED light bulbs may have a higher upfront cost but can result in substantial savings on utility bills.

Furthermore, exploring alternative options can be an effective strategy for mindful consumption. Instead of always buying brand-new items, consider purchasing pre-owned or refurbished goods. Not only does this save money, but it also extends the lifespan of resources and reduces waste. Thrift stores, online marketplaces for secondhand items, or local community swap events are great places to find high-quality used goods at a fraction of the cost.

Lastly, it is important to be proactive in seeking out sustainable and ethical brands that align with our values. Supporting companies that prioritize environmental stewardship, fair labor practices, and social responsibility not only contributes to a better world but also encourages others to follow suit. By consciously choosing to invest in ethical products and services, we send a powerful message that sustainability and responsibility matter.

By implementing these strategies for mindful consumption, we can make informed choices that align with the principles of Mottainai. Not only will we save money in the process, but we will also contribute to a more sustainable, fulfilling, and economically efficient lifestyle.

Budget-Friendly Options and Cost Benefits

In embracing the principles of Mottainai, one of the key benefits that individuals can experience is saving money through mindful consumption. By adopting a more conscious approach to our purchasing decisions, we can not only reduce waste but also find cost-effective alternatives to wasteful products and practices.

When it comes to everyday items, there are numerous budget-friendly options available that align with the principles of Mottainai. For example, instead of buying single-use plastic water bottles, investing in a durable and reusable water bottle can lead to significant savings over time. Similarly, opting for cloth napkins instead of disposable paper napkins not only reduces waste but also eliminates the recurring expense of purchasing disposable alternatives.

Another aspect of mindful consumption that offers cost benefits is reducing energy consumption. By being conscious of our energy usage and making simple changes like switching off lights when not in use or using energy-efficient appliances, we can lower our utility bills while minimizing our environmental impact.

Additionally, being mindful of the lifespan of our possessions can lead to significant cost savings. Instead of immediately replacing items that are damaged or broken, consider repairing them whenever possible. This not only saves money but also extends the lifespan of the item, reducing the need for new purchases.

Repurposing and upcycling existing items is another way to save money. Rather than throwing away old furniture or clothing, explore creative ways to give them a new life. For instance, transforming an old wooden pallet into a unique piece of furniture or converting old t-shirts into reusable shopping bags can save money while reducing waste.

In line with the principles of Mottainai, many communities have embraced the sharing economy as a means of reducing costs and maximizing resource utilization. Shared resources such as car-sharing, tool libraries, or community gardens provide affordable alternatives to individual ownership while promoting collaboration and community engagement.

By exploring these budget-friendly options and understanding the cost benefits associated with mindful resource utilization, individuals can not only save money but also contribute to a more sustainable future. The principles of Mottainai emphasize the importance of considering long-term value and durability when making purchasing decisions, ultimately leading to financial savings and a reduced environmental impact.

Extending the Lifespan of Possessions

One of the key aspects of Mottainai is the belief in getting the most out of what we possess. In today's throwaway culture, it's become all too easy to dispose of items at the first sign of wear or damage. However, by embracing Mottainai principles, we can shift our mindset and find creative solutions to extend the lifespan of our possessions.

Repairing, repurposing, and upcycling are powerful ways to breathe new life into old items and reduce waste. Instead of immediately discarding a broken item, take the time to assess if it can be repaired. Many repairs can be done at home, with countless tutorials available online for guidance. By learning basic repair skills or seeking the help of professionals, we can save money and prevent perfectly useful items from ending up in landfills.

Repurposing is another fantastic approach to make the most out of our possessions. Consider how an item can serve a new purpose instead of being discarded. For example, an old ladder can be transformed into a bookshelf, a glass jar can become a vase, or a wooden pallet can be turned into a stylish outdoor seating area. The possibilities are endless when we open our minds to creative repurposing ideas.

Upcycling takes repurposing to another level by transforming discarded objects into something entirely new and beautiful. By using our imagination and creativity, we can create stunning pieces of art or functional items from materials that would have otherwise been wasted. For instance, an old piece of furniture can be given a fresh coat of paint and upholstery to become a statement piece in our homes.

Inspiring examples abound of individuals and communities successfully extending the lifespan of possessions through these creative solutions. From community repair cafes where people come together to fix each other's belongings to social enterprises specializing in upcycled products, there is a growing movement dedicated to embracing Mottainai and reducing waste.

By extending the lifespan of our possessions, we not only

save money but also contribute to a more sustainable future. Repairing, repurposing, and upcycling are practical ways to reduce our environmental impact while embracing the values of Mottainai. Let us strive to see the potential in every item we own and discover the joy and satisfaction that comes from giving it a new lease on life.

The Role of Sharing Economy in Mottainai:

As we embrace the principles of Mottainai and seek to live more economically efficient lives, one powerful tool at our disposal is the sharing economy. The sharing economy refers to a system in which individuals share resources, either for free or for a fee, in order to optimize their usage and reduce waste. This concept aligns perfectly with Mottainai's philosophy of making the most out of what we possess.

Sharing economy platforms have gained significant popularity in recent years, revolutionizing various sectors and contributing to economic efficiency. These platforms provide opportunities for individuals to share or rent out possessions they no longer need on a temporary basis, rather than letting them go unused or engaging in unnecessary consumption.

One notable example of the sharing economy in action is car-sharing services. Instead of each individual owning a car that sits idle for the majority of the day, car-sharing platforms allow people to access vehicles on-demand, reducing the overall number of cars on the road and cutting down on the environmental and financial costs associated with car ownership. By embracing car-sharing services, individuals can save money on expenses like vehicle maintenance and insurance while still having access to transportation whenever they need it.

Tool libraries are another successful example of the sharing economy in practice. These community-based initiatives allow individuals to borrow tools and equipment for specific projects or tasks rather than buying them outright. By pooling resources and sharing tools, communities can reduce waste and save money, especially for items that are only needed occasionally. Tool libraries also foster a sense of community collaboration and resourcefulness, promoting the values inherent in Mottainai.

Additionally, sharing economy platforms have expanded into other sectors such as accommodation (e.g., home-sharing sites) and even skills exchanges (e.g., language learning platforms). These platforms empower individuals to utilize their resources efficiently while engaging with their communities in meaningful ways.

By incorporating sharing economy practices into our lives, we can tap into a vast reservoir of resources that might otherwise go to waste. It not only helps us save money but also encourages collaboration, strengthens social ties, and reduces the environmental impact of excessive consumption.

In the spirit of Mottainai, let us embrace the sharing economy and recognize the immense value in sharing and collectively optimizing our resources. By doing so, we contribute to economic efficiency, promote sustainability, and pave the way for a richer and more fulfilling future.

MOTTAINAI AND CULTURAL PRESERVATION: HONORING TRADITION THROUGH RESOURCE UTILIZATION

Cultural preservation plays a vital role in maintaining the unique identity and heritage of societies around the world. In today's globalized world, where cultures are constantly influenced by external forces, it becomes even more important to actively preserve these traditions.

One way to honor and protect our cultural heritage is through the practice of Mottainai. By embracing Mottainai principles, we can cultivate a deep sense of appreciation for traditional practices, materials, and artifacts, ensuring their continuity for future generations.

Cultural preservation holds immense significance as it allows us to maintain a connection with our roots and ancestral knowledge. It provides a sense of belonging and identity, fostering pride and unity within communities. Through Mottainai, we can actively engage in preserving cultural practices that may otherwise be at risk of disappearing.

Mottainai serves as a powerful tool for cultural revival. By adopting a mindful approach to resource utilization, we can support artisans, craftsmen, and traditional practitioners who play a crucial role in preserving our cultural traditions. Through their expertise and dedication, they keep alive the techniques and materials handed down through generations.

In exploring the role of Mottainai in cultural preservation, we discover inspiring examples where it has been successfully employed. Communities around the world have utilized Mottainai principles to revive ancient practices such as traditional weaving, pottery making, or woodwork. By valuing the resources available and avoiding waste, these communities have managed to sustain and promote their cultural heritage.

Art and craftsmanship also play a significant role in the preservation of culture. Many artisans embrace Mottainai by repurposing materials or utilizing traditional techniques to create beautiful artworks or functional objects deeply rooted in their cultural identity. By supporting these artisans, we contribute to the preservation of their craft and help maintain cultural diversity.

As important as cultural preservation is, it faces challenges in the modern world. Globalization, urbanization, and the fast-paced nature of contemporary life can often overshadow traditional practices, leading to their gradual decline. However, by incorporating Mottainai principles into cultural preservation efforts, we can find opportunities for collaboration and innovation.

The future of cultural preservation lies in finding ways to adapt and integrate traditional practices into our rapidly changing world. By embracing Mottainai, we can strike a balance between honoring tradition and adapting to modern needs. Collaboration between cultural preservation organizations and the Mottainai movement can create synergies that enhance sustainability and ensure the survival of our cultural heritage.

In the upcoming sections, we will explore case studies that showcase successful examples of cultural preservation through resource utilization and Mottainai principles. We will also delve into the role of art and craftsmanship in cultural revival efforts. Finally, we will examine the challenges faced by cultural preservation initiatives and highlight potential opportunities for collaboration in creating a sustainable future.

- Embracing Mottainai principles not only helps reduce waste but also plays a crucial role in the preservation and revival of cultural traditions. By recognizing the value in utilizing resources wisely and respecting the heritage behind them, we contribute to the ongoing tapestry of cultural diversity.

- Throughout history, communities around the world have relied on resource utilization as a means of preserving their cultural traditions. Mottainai provides a modern framework for this practice, emphasizing the importance of honoring the past while building a sustainable future.

- In Japan, various examples demonstrate the effectiveness of Mottainai in cultural preservation. From traditional textile production techniques passed down through generations to the careful restoration of historic buildings using salvaged materials, Mottainai serves as a tool for cultural revival.

- The success stories of communities embracing Mottainai principles are an inspiration to us all. Whether it's the revitalization of dying crafts, the preservation of endangered languages, or the revival of ancient rituals, these examples highlight the transformative power of Mottainai in preserving cultural heritage.

- While tangible artifacts and practices play a significant role in cultural preservation, art and craftsmanship also contribute to this process. Artists and craftsmen who embrace Mottainai principles find innovative ways to incorporate traditional elements into their creations, ensuring that cultural heritage remains relevant and appreciated by future generations.

- However, cultural preservation through Mottainai is not without its challenges. The modern world presents obstacles such as globalization, urbanization, and shifting demographics, which can pose threats to traditional practices. By understanding these challenges and seeking collaborative solutions, cultural preservation efforts can adapt and thrive.

- Opportunities exist for collaboration between cultural preservation initiatives and the Mottainai movement. By integrating Mottainai principles into cultural preservation strategies, we can create a synergy that fosters sustainable practices while safeguarding cultural heritage. This partnership opens up new avenues for education, community engagement, and economic development rooted in cultural authenticity.

- As we navigate the complexities of the modern world, embracing Mottainai for cultural preservation becomes increasingly vital. By valuing and utilizing resources with a mindful appreciation for their cultural significance, we ensure the continuity of diverse traditions and foster a sense of pride and identity within communities.

[Continued in Chapter 5...]

Case Studies: Celebrating Successful Cultural Preservation Efforts

Throughout history, cultures around the world have thrived on their unique traditions and practices. However, with the increasing globalization and modernization of society, many cultural traditions face the threat of being lost or forgotten. In this chapter, we celebrate the success stories of individuals, communities, and organizations that have effectively preserved cultural traditions through resource utilization and Mottainai principles. These case studies serve as an inspiration for others embarking on similar journeys.

1. Case Study: The Textile Artisans of Kutch, India

In the arid region of Kutch in India, a group of skilled textile artisans have successfully revived the dying art of bandhani and ajrakh printing. By embracing Mottainai principles and utilizing locally sourced organic materials, they have not only preserved centuries-old dyeing and printing techniques but also created sustainable livelihoods for themselves and their community. Through their commitment to traditional craftsmanship and resource conservation, they have put Kutch back on the global map as a hub for textile artistry.

2. Case Study: The Indigenous Communities of Canada's Pacific Northwest

The Indigenous communities living along the Pacific Northwest coast of Canada have long practiced sustainable resource utilization and cultural preservation. Through Mottainai principles deeply intertwined with their way of life, they have protected ancient traditions such as cedar bark weaving and totem carving. By passing down these skills from generation to generation and valuing the abundance of the natural world, these communities demonstrate the power of Mottainai in preserving cultural heritage.

3. Case Study: The Ogasawara Islands' Ecotourism Initiative

The Ogasawara Islands in Japan have successfully turned to ecotourism as a means of preserving their unique culture and environment. By adopting Mottainai principles in their tourism practices, local residents have protected the delicate ecosystem of the islands while sharing their cultural heritage with visitors.

From sustainable fishing practices to the utilization of traditional materials in architecture and crafts, the Ogasawara Islands serve as a shining example of how Mottainai can drive cultural preservation while promoting economic sustainability.

4. Case Study: The Haida Gwaii Rediscovery Program, Canada
The Haida Gwaii Rediscovery Program in Canada is dedicated to reviving Indigenous traditions and knowledge among the Haida people. Through resource utilization and a Mottainai-inspired approach, this community-led initiative has successfully reintroduced traditional practices such as carving cedar canoes, weaving cedar baskets, and preserving ancient oral histories. By centering their efforts on intergenerational learning and collaboration, the program is ensuring that Haida culture remains alive and flourishing for future generations.

These case studies represent just a handful of the countless successful cultural preservation efforts taking place worldwide. They demonstrate the transformative power of Mottainai principles in safeguarding cultural heritage while promoting sustainable living practices. By valuing and utilizing resources wisely, these individuals, communities, and organizations have become stewards of their cultural legacies, inspiring others to embark on similar journeys towards preserving and celebrating diverse traditions.

Preservation through Art and Craftsmanship

In our exploration of Mottainai and its connection to cultural preservation, it is essential to recognize the significant role that art and craftsmanship play in this endeavor. Art and craftsmanship serve as powerful mediums for not only preserving traditional practices but also for passing them on to future generations.

Art, in all its forms, has long been intertwined with culture. From paintings to sculptures, ceramics to textiles, each creation tells a story and reflects the essence of a particular time and place. By embracing Mottainai principles that prioritize resource utilization and minimize waste, artisans and craftsmen can contribute to the preservation of cultural heritage.

These skilled individuals demonstrate their commitment to tradition by utilizing Mottainai-inspired techniques to create traditional products or artworks. They embrace the idea of repurposing materials and breathing new life into what might otherwise be discarded. Through their work, they embody the spirit of Mottainai by recognizing the value in every resource and the significance of preserving cultural traditions.

For instance, let's take a closer look at a renowned ceramic artist named Hiroshi Minato. Based in Japan, Minato specializes in Bizen pottery, a traditional Japanese pottery technique dating back over 1,000 years. Bizen pottery is known for its earthy tones, unique textures, and distinct firing process that relies solely on wood-burning kilns.

Minato exemplifies Mottainai principles in his craft by meticulously selecting clay from local sources and repurposing leftover materials from previous projects. He believes in giving new life to discarded fragments and transforming them into exquisite pieces of art. By embracing Mottainai, Minato not only honors the tradition of Bizen pottery but also respects the finite resources of our planet.

Another compelling example is the art of kintsugi, which involves repairing broken pottery with lacquer mixed with powdered gold, silver, or platinum. This method highlights the beauty in imperfections, paying homage to the history and story of each piece. By embracing Mottainai principles, kintsugi artisans prioritize resourcefulness and extend the lifespan of damaged pottery, rather than discarding it.

These examples of artisans and craftsmen utilizing Mottainai principles showcase the deep respect they hold for their cultural heritage. By using their creativity and technical skills, they preserve traditional practices while also adapting them to suit contemporary tastes and demands. Through their art, they bridge the gap between past and present, reviving cultural traditions for future generations to appreciate and cherish.

As we explore the intersection of Mottainai and cultural preservation, it is crucial to recognize and celebrate the role that art and craftsmanship play in this process. These skilled individuals honor tradition by repurposing materials, breathing new life into discarded fragments, and creating beautiful works that embody the spirit of Mottainai. Through their dedication to preserving cultural heritage, they inspire us all to embrace the transformative power of Mottainai in our own lives.

Future Challenges and Opportunities in Cultural Preservation through Mottainai

As cultural preservation efforts continue to evolve in the modern world, there are several challenges that need to be addressed to ensure the sustainability of these initiatives. By understanding these challenges and exploring potential opportunities, we can forge a path forward that combines the power of cultural preservation with the principles of Mottainai for a more sustainable future.

One of the key challenges in cultural preservation is the risk of cultural erosion and loss of traditional knowledge. In an increasingly globalized world, traditional practices and customs often face the threat of being overshadowed by Western influences or fading away due to lack of interest among younger generations. To combat this challenge, incorporating Mottainai principles can be instrumental in rekindling interest and appreciation for traditional cultures.

Another challenge is the lack of resources and funding for cultural preservation projects. Many cultural institutions and heritage sites struggle to secure sufficient financial support to maintain and protect their valuable artifacts and traditions. By adopting Mottainai principles, including resource utilization and waste reduction, these initiatives can become more sustainable and cost-effective. For example, repurposing existing materials or utilizing traditional techniques can help reduce expenses while still preserving cultural heritage.

Furthermore, there is a need for stronger collaboration between cultural preservation organizations and the Mottainai movement. By joining forces, these two movements can create synergistic opportunities for mutual benefit. Cultural preservation efforts can benefit from incorporating Mottainai principles such as sustainable resource management, while the Mottainai movement can draw inspiration from traditional practices and promote their preservation.

Additionally, embracing technology and digital platforms can provide new avenues for cultural preservation through Mottainai. With the advent of virtual reality, augmented reality, and online repositories, it is now possible to digitally preserve cultural artifacts, traditions, and knowledge. These technological advancements not only help overcome geographical limitations but also offer interactive experiences that can engage a wider audience in cultural preservation efforts.

Moreover, education plays a crucial role in preserving cultural heritage. Integrating Mottainai principles into educational curricula at various levels can instill values of conservation and sustainability in the next generation. By fostering an appreciation for traditional practices and the importance of resource utilization early on, we can ensure that cultural preservation becomes ingrained in society's consciousness.

In conclusion, while cultural preservation faces challenges in the modern world, combining Mottainai principles with these efforts presents numerous opportunities for a sustainable future.

By addressing the risk of cultural erosion, securing resources for preservation projects, fostering collaboration between cultural preservation and Mottainai movements, embracing technology, and prioritizing education, we can create a harmonious balance that honors tradition while promoting a more mindful and sustainable world.

FROM DISPOSABLE TO DURABLE: EMBRACING LONG-LASTING PRODUCTS IN A THROWAWAY SOCIETY

As we navigate through our modern consumer-driven society, it becomes increasingly evident that we live in a culture of disposability. We are constantly bombarded with advertisements and encouraged to purchase the latest products, only to discard them shortly after in favor of the next trendy item. This culture of disposability has profound consequences for our environment and contributes to the mounting waste crisis we face today.

The negative impact of this disposable mindset cannot be underestimated. Every year, millions of tons of products end up in landfills, releasing harmful greenhouse gases and toxic substances into the environment. The short lifespan of these products not only leads to wasted resources but also exacerbates the depletion of natural reserves and intensifies the demand for more production, perpetuating a vicious cycle of waste and environmental degradation.

It is crucial that we recognize the urgency of addressing this issue and shift our mindset towards embracing durable products.

Unlike their disposable counterparts, durable products offer many benefits that extend beyond their longevity. By opting for durable goods, we can significantly reduce waste generation, conserve valuable resources, and mitigate the harmful environmental impacts associated with excessive consumption.

Furthermore, durable products often exhibit superior quality, craftsmanship, and materials compared to their disposable counterparts. They are designed to withstand the test of time and frequent use, making them more reliable and cost-effective in the long run. By investing in durable products, we can break free from the throwaway mentality and embrace a more sustainable approach to our consumer habits.

In the following chapters, we will explore strategies for choosing long-lasting products, the importance of maintenance and repair in prolonging product lifespans, and the transformative power of changing consumer habits and mindset. Together, let us embark on a journey towards a world where durability is valued over disposability, and where every purchase contributes to a sustainable future.

The Benefits of Embracing Durable Products

In our modern throwaway society, the culture of disposability has become deeply ingrained. We are constantly bombarded with advertisements and trends that encourage us to replace our belongings frequently, leading to a mindset of immediate gratification and an alarming increase in waste generation. However, by embracing durable products, we can counteract this detrimental trend and make a significant impact on both our personal lives and the environment.

Durable products are designed to withstand the test of time, offering longevity and value that surpasses their disposable counterparts. Unlike items that quickly wear out or become obsolete, durable products are built to last, reducing the need for frequent replacements and ultimately minimizing waste production. By investing in durable products, we can foster sustainability and resource conservation in several key ways.

Firstly, durable products contribute to a significant reduction in resource consumption. Producing and disposing of goods consumes vast amounts of energy, water, and raw materials, all of which have serious environmental implications. When we choose durable products, we decrease the demand for new items and lessen the strain on our planet's resources. This means fewer carbon emissions, decreased water usage, and reduced extraction of nonrenewable materials.

Secondly, embracing durable products helps combat the growing issue of electronic waste. With technology advancing at a rapid pace, it is common for electronic devices like smartphones and laptops to become outdated within a few years. This constant cycle of upgrading leads to an alarming accumulation of electronic waste, which is not only harmful to the environment but also poses health risks due to toxic components. By opting for durable electronics that are designed for long-term use and upgradability, we can significantly reduce electronic waste and contribute to a more sustainable future.

Furthermore, choosing durable products often results in financial savings in the long run. While durable products may have a higher upfront cost compared to their disposable counterparts, their extended lifespan offsets this initial investment. When we consider the costs of repeatedly replacing low-quality items, it becomes clear that durable products provide better value over time. By investing in quality and durability, we can save money in the long term while reducing waste simultaneously.

Moreover, embracing durable products encourages a shift in our consumer mentality. Instead of succumbing to the allure of novelty and instant gratification, we begin to prioritize long-term value and mindful consumption. This shift not only benefits us personally but also cultivates a more sustainable and responsible society. By valuing durability over disposability, we become conscious consumers who take into account the environmental impact and longevity of our purchases.

In summary, embracing durable products offers numerous benefits for both individuals and the environment. By choosing quality over quantity and investing in items built to last, we contribute to sustainability, resource conservation, and financial savings. The concept of embracing durable products aligns perfectly with Mottainai principles by promoting thoughtful resource utilization and inspiring a shift towards a culture of longevity. By adopting this mindset, we can play an active role in creating a more sustainable future for ourselves and generations to come.

Strategies for Choosing Long-lasting Products

To truly embrace the concept of Mottainai and shift away from our throwaway society, it is crucial to make conscious choices when it comes to selecting long-lasting products. By investing in items that are built to last and considering factors such as quality, materials, and craftsmanship, we can significantly reduce waste and contribute to a more sustainable future. Here are some strategies to help you choose durable products in various categories:

1. Clothing:
- Look for well-constructed garments made from high-quality materials. Opt for natural fibers like organic cotton, linen, or wool, as they tend to be more durable than synthetic fabrics.
- Check the stitching and seams to ensure they are sturdy and reinforced.
- Consider timeless styles that won't go out of fashion quickly, allowing you to wear the clothing for years to come.

2. Appliances:

- Research brands known for their durability and reliability. Read reviews from other consumers who have used the products over an extended period.
- Pay attention to the warranty offered by the manufacturer. A longer warranty often indicates confidence in the product's longevity.
- Consider energy-efficient appliances, as they not only save you money on utility bills but also tend to be better built and last longer.

3. Furniture:
- Choose furniture pieces made from solid wood or high-quality materials. Avoid particleboard or low-grade plywood, as they are less durable.
- Examine the construction of the furniture, including joints and connections. Well-built furniture should have sturdy joints held together with dowels, screws, or mortise and tenon.
- Look for furniture that can be easily repaired or refinished, allowing it to adapt to your changing needs and style preferences.

It's important to note that choosing durable products may require a higher upfront investment compared to disposable alternatives. However, the long-term value and reduced environmental impact make it a worthwhile choice. By carefully considering the quality, materials, and craftsmanship of the items we bring into our lives, we can actively contribute to breaking free from the culture of disposability and embracing a lifestyle rooted in Mottainai principles.

Extending the Lifespan of Products through Maintenance and Repair

One of the key elements in embracing durable products and shifting away from a throwaway society is the importance of proper maintenance to prolong the life of our belongings. By taking care of the items we own, we can significantly reduce waste and contribute to a more sustainable future.

The concept of maintenance is often overlooked in our fast-paced consumer culture, where the focus is on acquiring new things rather than preserving what we already have. However, by investing time and effort into maintaining our possessions, we can extend their lifespan and derive greater value from them.

To begin with, it's essential to understand that maintenance goes beyond basic cleanliness. While keeping items clean is an important aspect, maintenance also involves regular inspections, repairs, and preventive measures. By addressing minor issues early on, we can prevent further damage and ensure that our belongings continue to function optimally.

There are various resources available for repair and maintenance, catering to different needs and skill levels. DIY options are excellent for those who have the expertise or are willing to learn. Countless online tutorials, repair manuals, and forums provide valuable information and guidance on fixing common issues with different types of products. Engaging in DIY repairs not only saves money but also empowers individuals with practical skills and a sense of accomplishment.

For more complex repairs or situations where expert knowledge is required, professional repair services are readily available. Many businesses specialize in repairing specific products such as electronics, appliances, or furniture. These professionals have the necessary expertise and tools to diagnose and fix problems efficiently. By utilizing their services, we can breathe new life into our belongings and avoid premature disposal.

In recent years, community repair initiatives have gained popularity as well. These initiatives often take the form of repair cafes or workshops where volunteers with repair skills come together to assist individuals in fixing their broken items. These events create a supportive environment for learning, sharing knowledge, and fostering a sense of community. Participating in such initiatives not only helps us extend the lifespan of our products but also promotes a culture of sharing skills and resources within our communities.

By embracing maintenance and repair practices, we can challenge the throwaway mentality that dominates our society. Taking care of our belongings demonstrates a commitment to sustainable living, resulting in reduced waste, resource conservation, and financial savings. Furthermore, it encourages a shift from passive consumption to active engagement with our possessions.

In conclusion, extending the lifespan of products through maintenance and repair is an essential aspect of embracing durable items in a throwaway society. By prioritizing regular inspections, repairs, and preventive measures, we can significantly reduce waste and contribute to a more sustainable future. Whether through DIY efforts, professional repair services, or community initiatives, there are ample resources available to help us maintain and prolong the life of our belongings. Let us embrace these practices to create a world where the value of durability is cherished and waste is minimized.

Changing Consumer Habits and Mindset:

In a world dominated by fast fashion, disposable electronics, and single-use products, embracing durable alternatives requires a fundamental shift in consumer mentality. It means moving away from the allure of immediate gratification and towards a mindset that prioritizes long-term value. So how can we change our consumer habits and mindset to embrace the idea of durable products?

Firstly, it is important to understand the benefits, both personal and environmental, that come with adopting a more mindful approach to purchasing decisions. By investing in quality, long-lasting products, we not only reduce waste but also save money in the long run. Durability means fewer replacements and repairs, ultimately leading to significant cost savings over time.

Additionally, choosing durable products goes hand-in-hand with the principles of Mottainai. It allows us to fully appreciate the resources that went into creating those products and honors the efforts of the individuals who designed and crafted them. By valuing durability over disposability, we break free from the cycle of mindless consumption and instead make mindful choices that align with our values.

Changing consumer habits also involves conducting thorough research and becoming informed consumers. This includes reading reviews, researching materials and manufacturing processes, and considering factors such as product quality, craftsmanship, and warranty. By taking the time to make informed decisions, we can ensure that our purchases align with our values and contribute to a more sustainable future.

Another important aspect of changing consumer habits is recognizing the power of our choices. Each purchase we make sends a message to companies and manufacturers about what we, as consumers, value. By consciously choosing durable products, we not only support businesses that prioritize sustainability but also create a demand for better alternatives.

Furthermore, developing a mindset of durability encourages us to take responsibility for the items we own. It emphasizes the importance of proper maintenance to extend the lifespan of products. By caring for our belongings and repairing them when necessary, we actively participate in the movement towards a more sustainable and resourceful society.

In conclusion, embracing durable products requires a shift in consumer habits and mindset. By valuing long-term value over immediate gratification, conducting thorough research, and taking responsibility for the items we own, we can make mindful choices that align with our values and contribute to a more sustainable future. This shift not only benefits the environment but also brings personal fulfillment as we embrace a lifestyle rooted in Mottainai principles.

LESSONS FROM NATURE: APPLYING MOTTAINAI PRINCIPLES TO ENVIRONMENTAL CONSERVATION

Understanding Nature's Cyclical Processes:

In this chapter, we delve into the intricate and awe-inspiring cycles and systems that sustain our planet. From the water cycle to the carbon cycle and nutrient cycling, these natural processes serve as a profound source of inspiration for practicing Mottainai in environmental conservation.

The water cycle, for instance, showcases the continuous movement and transformation of water on Earth. Through evaporation, condensation, precipitation, and runoff, water replenishes our rivers, lakes, and oceans, providing life-sustaining resources to countless organisms. By understanding and appreciating the importance of this cycle, we can cultivate a deep respect for water as a precious resource and actively work towards its preservation.

Similarly, the carbon cycle highlights the essential role of carbon in maintaining Earth's delicate balance. From photosynthesis by plants to respiration by animals and decomposition by microorganisms, carbon moves through various stages within the biosphere, geosphere, hydrosphere, and atmosphere. Recognizing the significance of this cycle can inspire us to minimize carbon emissions and promote practices that sequester carbon, such as reforestation and sustainable land management.

Additionally, nutrient cycling highlights the intricate processes by which essential elements like nitrogen and phosphorus are recycled within ecosystems. From their uptake by plants to consumption by animals and subsequent decomposition by decomposers, nutrients continuously circulate through the environment, nourishing life at every level. Understanding the importance of nutrient cycling can encourage us to adopt regenerative agricultural practices that promote soil health and reduce reliance on synthetic fertilizers.

By immersing ourselves in these natural cycles and systems, we gain a profound appreciation for their inherent wisdom and efficiency. They demonstrate the power of interconnectedness and remind us of our role as stewards of the Earth. As we embrace Mottainai principles in environmental conservation, let us draw inspiration from nature's cyclical processes to create sustainable solutions that preserve our planet's delicate balance.

Composting: Transforming Waste into Nutrient-Rich Soil:

When it comes to environmental conservation, one of the most effective practices that aligns perfectly with the principles of Mottainai is composting. Composting allows us to transform organic waste into nutrient-rich soil, providing a sustainable solution for waste reduction and soil fertility enhancement.

The process of composting involves creating an environment where microorganisms can break down organic materials such as food scraps, yard waste, and plant trimmings. By providing the right conditions, including a proper balance of carbon-rich (also known as "brown") materials like dried leaves or shredded paper, and nitrogen-rich (or "green") materials like fruit peels or grass clippings, the microorganisms can thrive and efficiently decompose the waste.

There are several benefits to composting that make it a crucial practice in reducing landfill waste and enriching soil fertility. Firstly, by diverting organic waste from landfills, we minimize the production of harmful greenhouse gases, particularly methane. Methane is a potent greenhouse gas that contributes to climate change, so by composting instead of landfilling organic waste, we can significantly reduce our carbon footprint.

Furthermore, composting allows us to create nutrient-rich soil amendment that can be used in gardening and agriculture. The finished compost adds valuable organic matter to the soil, improving its structure, water-holding capacity, and nutrient content. This means healthier plants, reduced reliance on synthetic fertilizers, and improved overall soil health.

To start your own compost pile or use compost bins, follow these simple steps:

1. Choose a suitable location: Find a spot in your backyard or garden where you can set up your compost pile or bin. It should be conveniently accessible yet not too close to your living spaces.

2. Gather compostable materials: Collect a variety of organic materials such as fruit and vegetable scraps, coffee grounds, tea bags, eggshells, yard waste like leaves and grass clippings, and even small amounts of paper products like shredded newspaper or cardboard.

3. Create layers: Begin with a layer of brown materials, then alternate with green materials. Aim for a 2:1 ratio of brown to green materials. This balance helps maintain optimal conditions for decomposition and prevents the pile from becoming too wet or

smelly.

4. Maintain moisture and aeration: Keep the compost pile moist, similar to a damp sponge. If it gets too dry, water it gently. Turn the pile occasionally with a pitchfork or compost aerator to introduce air into the mix, aiding in the decomposition process.

5. Monitor and adjust: Regularly check the moisture level and temperature of your compost pile, aiming for a slightly warm interior that indicates active decomposition. Adjust the carbon-to-nitrogen ratio if necessary by adding more brown or green materials accordingly.

6. Harvest and use the compost: After several months, your compost will transform into dark, crumbly soil-like material. This signifies that it's ready to be used as a nutrient-rich amendment for your garden beds, potted plants, or lawn.

By incorporating composting into our daily lives, we not only reduce waste and support environmental conservation but also create valuable resources that benefit our gardens and ecosystems. The act of transforming organic waste into nutrient-rich soil is a practical way to embrace Mottainai principles and contribute to a more sustainable future.

Rewilding: Restoring Balance and Biodiversity in Ecosystems:

Rewilding is a powerful conservation approach that aims to restore balance and biodiversity in ecosystems by reintroducing native species, removing barriers to natural processes, and creating suitable habitats for wildlife. By emulating the natural processes that shaped landscapes for millennia, rewilding presents a promising solution for addressing the ecological challenges of our time.

One notable example of successful rewilding is the reintroduction of wolves into Yellowstone National Park in the United States. Wolves had been hunted to extinction in the park by the early

1900s, resulting in an overabundance of herbivores such as elk. Without natural predators, the elk population grew unchecked, leading to overgrazing of vegetation and consequent changes in the ecosystem.

In 1995, wolves were reintroduced into Yellowstone, and the effects were profound. The presence of wolves triggered what ecologists call a "trophic cascade," a ripple effect through various levels of the food chain. As the wolf population increased, elk behavior changed. They became more cautious and avoided areas where they were vulnerable to predation. This allowed vegetation, such as willows and aspens, to recover, providing habitat for beavers and other species.

With the return of these key species, riparian areas rejuvenated, leading to increased biodiversity and improved water quality. Birds nested in the newly available habitat, and fish populations thrived as streamside vegetation stabilized banks and reduced erosion. The rewilding of Yellowstone demonstrates how the reintroduction of just one species can have cascading benefits for an entire ecosystem.

Inspired by this success, rewilding projects have been implemented across the globe in diverse landscapes. One example is the Oostvaardersplassen nature reserve in the Netherlands. Formerly reclaimed land used for agriculture, it has been transformed into a rich wetland habitat attracting numerous bird species and large herbivores like Konik horses and Heck cattle. This rewilding initiative has not only created a unique habitat for wildlife but has also become a popular destination for eco-tourism, benefiting the local economy.

Individuals can play an active role in supporting rewilding initiatives within their local communities. They can participate in citizen science projects that monitor and document biodiversity, volunteer for habitat restoration efforts, or support local organizations working towards rewilding goals. By spreading awareness about the importance of rewilding and advocating for its implementation on a larger scale, individuals can contribute to the restoration of balance and biodiversity in ecosystems.

Rewilding serves as a reminder of the intricate interconnections between species and the importance of restoring natural processes. By embracing the principles of rewilding, we can create healthier, more resilient ecosystems that benefit both wildlife and people. Through our collective efforts, we have the power to restore harmony and balance to our planet, one rewilding project at a time.

Regenerative Agriculture: Nurturing the Soil for Sustainable Food Production:

In this section, we delve into the concept of regenerative agriculture and its profound connection to Mottainai principles. Regenerative agriculture goes beyond conventional farming methods by focusing on nurturing the soil and promoting biodiversity, leading to sustainable food production and environmental conservation.

We explore various techniques employed in regenerative agriculture, such as cover cropping, crop rotation, and agroforestry. By incorporating these practices, farmers can enhance soil health, conserve water, and reduce the need for chemical inputs. This not only benefits the environment but also increases the resilience of agricultural systems in the face of climate change.

Through inspiring examples from around the world, we showcase how regenerative agriculture has yielded positive outcomes for both farmers and the planet. From improving soil fertility and increasing crop yields to sequestering carbon and mitigating greenhouse gas emissions, regenerative agriculture offers a holistic approach to sustainable food production.

We highlight the importance of supporting farmers who embrace regenerative practices by making conscious choices in our consumption habits. By opting for organic, locally sourced produce and supporting farmer's markets or Community Supported Agriculture (CSA) programs, we contribute to the growth of regenerative agriculture and its positive impact on our food systems.

The section concludes with practical tips on how readers can incorporate regenerative agriculture principles into their own lives. Whether it be starting a small-scale garden, advocating for sustainable agricultural policies, or volunteering at local farms, individuals can play an active role in promoting regenerative practices and contributing to a more sustainable future.

By embracing regenerative agriculture as an integral part of Mottainai principles, we align ourselves with nature's wisdom and become catalysts for positive change. Through nurturing the soil, conserving water, and prioritizing biodiversity, we forge a path towards a more resilient and sustainable future for both ourselves and future generations.

Harmonizing with Nature: Living in Sync with Natural Rhythms

In this section, we invite readers to embrace the natural rhythms of nature and align their lifestyles accordingly. By living in harmony with the Earth's cycles, we not only benefit the environment but also experience personal well-being and fulfillment.

One way to harmonize with nature is through seasonal eating. This practice involves consuming fruits, vegetables, and other foods that are locally and seasonally available. By doing so, we support local farmers, reduce the carbon footprint associated with long-distance transportation, and enjoy produce at its peak freshness and nutritional value. Incorporating seasonal eating into our lives can be as simple as visiting farmers markets or joining community-supported agriculture (CSA) programs to access locally grown fruits and vegetables.

Conserving energy during peak demand times is another way to harmonize with natural rhythms. Peak electricity demand often occurs during certain hours of the day when individuals are using electrical appliances simultaneously. By shifting some of our energy usage to off-peak hours or implementing energy-saving practices, such as turning off lights when not in use or using energy-efficient appliances, we can reduce strain on the electrical grid and minimize our carbon footprint.

Respecting wildlife habitats is also essential for living in harmony with nature. By understanding and appreciating the ecosystems around us, we can make conscious choices to protect and preserve wildlife habitats. This may involve refraining from activities that disrupt or harm natural habitats, such as avoiding excessive noise pollution near nesting areas or refraining from feeding wild animals in ways that can harm their health or natural behaviors.

To incorporate these principles into daily life, we offer practical tips and suggestions. Examples include creating a seasonal meal plan that utilizes locally available ingredients, adjusting daily routines to prioritize energy conservation during peak demand periods, and taking steps to create wildlife-friendly spaces in our own backyards by planting native plants and providing habitat structures like bird feeders or nest boxes.

Living in sync with the natural rhythms of nature not only connects us more deeply to the world around us but also enables us to contribute to environmental sustainability. By embracing Mottainai principles in our daily lives and harmonizing with nature, we can create a positive impact on both a personal and global scale.

MINDFUL CONSUMPTION HABITS: CULTIVATING AWARENESS AND GRATITUDE IN EVERYDAY LIFE

The Power of Mindful Consumption

In this chapter, we explore the concept of mindful consumption and its profound connection to Mottainai principles. Mindful consumption is about cultivating awareness and intentionality in our consumption habits, allowing us to make conscious choices that align with our values and have a positive impact on both ourselves and the world around us.

Mindful consumption starts with a heightened awareness of our own desires, needs, and motivations when it comes to acquiring and using resources. It encourages us to question the impulse of constantly wanting more and instead focus on what truly brings us contentment and fulfillment. By slowing down and reflecting on our consumption patterns, we can uncover the underlying reasons behind our desires and make conscious decisions that align with our values.

One key aspect of practicing mindful consumption is considering the lifecycle of the products we bring into our lives. From production to disposal, every item we consume has an environmental impact. By being mindful of this impact, we can strive to make choices that minimize harm to the planet. This involves considering factors such as the materials used, the manufacturing processes involved, and the durability and longevity of the product.

Mindful consumption also encompasses ethical considerations. We can choose to support brands and businesses that prioritize fair trade practices, sustainable sourcing, and social responsibility. By aligning our values with our purchasing decisions, we become agents of change, encouraging businesses to adopt more sustainable and ethical practices.

Another important aspect of mindful consumption is reducing waste. We can minimize our environmental footprint by opting for reusable alternatives, repairing items instead of discarding them, and embracing a circular economy mindset. Rather than succumbing to the throwaway culture that dominates modern society, we can choose to extend the life cycle of products by repurposing or upcycling them. By doing so, we not only reduce waste but also tap into our creativity and find joy in giving new life to old objects.

Cultivating a sense of gratitude is also at the core of mindful consumption. By appreciating the resources that are available to us, we develop a deeper connection with the items we consume. We can express gratitude for the sustenance provided by our food, the functionality offered by our tools, and the beauty created by our possessions. This shift in perspective helps us recognize the abundance in our lives and fosters a greater sense of contentment.

In essence, practicing mindful consumption is about being present in our everyday choices and taking responsibility for the impact of those choices. It empowers us to prioritize quality over quantity, align our actions with our values, and find fulfillment in living a more intentional and sustainable life. By embracing mindful consumption, we embody the essence of Mottainai and contribute to a happier, richer, and more fulfilled existence.

Developing mindfulness in consumption choices is an essential aspect of embracing Mottainai principles and cultivating a more fulfilled life. In this section, we will explore specific strategies and techniques to help readers develop mindfulness in their everyday consumption decisions.

1. Engage in Pause and Reflect Practice:
One effective strategy for developing mindfulness in consumption choices is to practice pausing and reflecting before making any purchase or consuming any resource. Take a moment to consider the necessity of the item or resource and whether it aligns with your values and goals. This practice allows you to become aware of your intentions behind the consumption and make conscious choices that are in line with your values.

2. Consider the Lifecycle of the Product:
Another important element of mindful consumption is considering the entire lifecycle of the product, from its creation to its eventual disposal. Before making a purchase, reflect on the environmental impact of the product's production, packaging, transportation, and potential waste it may generate. By understanding the lifecycle of the product, you can make informed decisions about whether it aligns with your commitment to sustainability.

3. Embrace Minimalism:
Practicing minimalism can be a powerful tool for developing mindfulness in consumption choices. Minimalism encourages individuals to focus on quality over quantity and prioritize meaningful experiences over material possessions. By adopting a minimalist mindset, you become more intentional with

your consumption, avoiding unnecessary purchases, and only acquiring items that truly add value to your life.

4. Explore Alternative Consumption Models:
In addition to practicing minimalism, consider exploring alternative consumption models such as sharing economy platforms or second-hand markets. These options allow you to extend the lifespan of products by giving them new life through reuse or sharing. By engaging in these alternative consumption models, you not only reduce waste but also support a more sustainable and mindful approach to resource utilization.

5. Cultivate Self-Awareness:
Self-awareness is a key component of developing mindfulness in consumption choices. Take time to examine your own consumption patterns and reflect on the underlying motivations behind them. Are your consumption habits driven by genuine needs or societal pressures? By understanding your own consumption triggers, you can make conscious choices that align with your values and avoid mindless consumption.

6. Practice Gratitude for Resources:
Cultivating a mindset of gratitude towards the resources you consume is an essential aspect of mindful consumption. Acknowledge and appreciate the value and impact of each item in your life, recognizing the resources and effort that went into its creation. By practicing gratitude, you develop a deeper appreciation for what you possess, reducing the desire for excessive consumption and wastefulness.

By incorporating these strategies into your daily life, you can develop mindfulness in your consumption choices, making conscious decisions that align with your values and contribute to a more sustainable and fulfilled existence. Remember, every choice matters, and embracing mindfulness in consumption is a powerful step towards living in harmony with Mottainai principles.

Practicing Gratitude for Resources

In this section, we delve into the importance of cultivating a mindset of gratitude towards the resources we have and the impact they have on our lives. In a world where overconsumption and waste are rampant, it is crucial to pause and appreciate the value and significance of the items we possess.

Gratitude is a powerful practice that can bring about a shift in perspective and transform our relationship with the things we own. When we express gratitude for the resources available to us, we begin to recognize their true worth and value. This mindfulness allows us to fully appreciate the effort, energy, and resources that went into producing these items.

One way to cultivate gratitude is by taking the time to reflect on the journey of each possession. Consider the origin of an item, from its raw materials to its manufacturing process. Reflect on the skill, craftsmanship, and creativity involved in creating it. Acknowledge the resources and labor that were utilized, as well as the impact these processes may have had on the environment.

By developing an understanding of the interconnectedness between resources, labor, and consumption, we gain a deeper appreciation for what we own. We start to see possessions not just as objects but as reminders of the complex web of relationships that sustain our lifestyles.

Another practice to cultivate gratitude is to regularly express appreciation for the items we use. Whether it's a simple thank you or a moment of reflection, acknowledging the role each possession plays in our lives fosters a sense of reverence and respect. By consciously expressing gratitude for our possessions, we elevate them from mere objects to sources of joy, functionality, and inspiration.

Gratitude extends beyond material possessions as well. It

encompasses intangible resources such as time, energy, knowledge, and relationships. By recognizing and appreciating these non-material resources, we develop a holistic view of gratitude that extends beyond material accumulation.

Cultivating gratitude for resources not only fosters a deeper sense of fulfillment and contentment, but it also encourages us to use these resources responsibly. When we are aware of the value of what we own, we are more likely to take care of our possessions and extend their lifespan. This mindset aligns with the core principles of Mottainai, as it promotes mindful consumption and a commitment to reducing waste.

As we move forward in our journey towards embracing Mottainai, let us remember the importance of practicing gratitude for the resources available to us. By cultivating a mindset of appreciation and awareness, we not only enrich our own lives but also contribute to a more sustainable and mindful world.

-----

4. Mindful Eating: Nourishing Our Bodies and the Planet
In this section, we dive into the practice of mindful eating and its profound benefits for personal health and environmental sustainability. Mindful eating involves being fully present and engaged with our food, savoring each bite, and cultivating a deeper connection to the nourishment it provides.

By adopting mindful eating practices, we can not only enhance our overall well-being but also reduce food waste and minimize our ecological footprint. Here are some key points to consider:

1. Savoring Food: The act of savoring food involves engaging all our senses while eating. By slowing down and appreciating the flavors, textures, and aromas of our meals, we develop a greater appreciation for the nourishment they provide. This mindful approach to eating also allows us to listen to our bodies' hunger and satiety cues, helping us make more balanced food choices.

2. Reducing Waste: Mindful eating goes hand in hand with reducing food waste. By paying attention to portion sizes, planning meals ahead, and utilizing leftovers creatively, we can minimize the amount of food that goes to waste. Through thoughtful meal planning and storage strategies, we can also extend the shelf life of perishable items, reducing the need for constant grocery shopping.

3. Conscious Food Choices: Being mindful of the impact of our food choices on both our health and the planet is an essential aspect of sustainable eating. By opting for locally sourced, seasonal produce, we support local farmers and reduce the carbon footprint associated with long-distance transportation. Choosing organic and ethically produced foods also contributes to a healthier environment by minimizing pesticide use and supporting sustainable farming practices.

4. Minimizing Packaging Waste: Mindful eating extends beyond just the food itself; it encompasses the packaging and waste generated by our consumption habits. When grocery shopping, we can prioritize products with minimal packaging or opt for bulk options to reduce single-use plastic waste. By being conscious consumers, we can encourage companies to adopt more sustainable packaging practices.

By embracing mindful eating, we tap into the power of gratitude and appreciation for the nourishment our food provides. Through conscious choices and a deeper connection to our meals, we not only nourish our bodies but also contribute to a healthier planet.

Mindful Shopping: Making Informed Choices

When it comes to our consumption habits, shopping plays a significant role. From groceries to clothing, we are constantly making choices about what we bring into our lives. By approaching shopping mindfully, we can make informed decisions that align with Mottainai principles and contribute to a happier, richer, and more fulfilled life.

One aspect of mindful shopping is considering the ethical sourcing of the items we purchase. This means taking into account the environmental and social impact of production processes. Before buying a product, consider researching the company's values and practices. Look for brands that prioritize sustainability, fair trade, and workers' rights. By supporting ethical brands, we can vote with our wallets and contribute to positive change.

Durability is another important factor to consider when shopping mindfully. Instead of opting for cheaply made items that may need frequent replacement, invest in products built to last. Look for high-quality materials and craftsmanship that ensure longevity. Not only does this reduce waste, but it also saves money in the long run. Remember the old saying, "Buy once, buy well."

Necessity is also key when it comes to mindful shopping. Before making a purchase, ask yourself if the item is truly essential or if it is simply a fleeting desire. Avoid falling into the trap of impulse buying and instead take time to reflect on whether the item aligns with your values and serves a purpose in your life. By adopting a mindful approach to shopping, we can resist the allure of unnecessary consumption.

Reducing packaging waste is another consideration for mindful shoppers. Choose products with minimal or recyclable packaging whenever possible. Bring reusable bags or containers when you go shopping to minimize the use of single-use plastics. Additionally, consider purchasing in bulk to reduce individual packaging waste. By being conscious of packaging, we contribute to waste reduction efforts and the preservation of our planet.

Incorporating these tips into our shopping habits allows us to make a positive impact on both our lives and the planet. By considering ethical sourcing, durability, necessity, and packaging waste, we align our choices with Mottainai principles and embrace a mindful approach to consumption. Let's remember that we have the power to vote for a more sustainable and compassionate future every time we make a purchase.

EMBRACING MINIMALISM: DECLUTTERING AND SIMPLIFYING FOR A MORE FULFILLED LIFE

In this chapter, we explore the benefits of embracing minimalism and the positive impacts it can have on our lives. By adopting a minimalist lifestyle, individuals can experience increased mental clarity, improved focus, reduced stress, and enhanced overall well-being.

One of the key advantages of minimalism is the ability to create space for what truly matters. By decluttering our living spaces and simplifying our possessions, we free ourselves from the burden of excess stuff. This newfound space allows us to breathe easier and creates an environment that promotes calmness and tranquility.

Minimalism also helps us cultivate a sense of freedom. When we let go of material possessions that no longer serve a purpose or bring us joy, we are liberated from the weight of our belongings. We become less attached to physical objects and find freedom in living with less.

Contentment is another benefit of embracing minimalism. By focusing on what truly brings us happiness and fulfillment, we learn to appreciate the simple joys in life. It encourages us to shift our mindset away from constantly seeking more and instead find contentment in what we already have.

Furthermore, minimalism contributes to a more sustainable and environmentally conscious lifestyle. By reducing our consumption and prioritizing quality over quantity, we help minimize waste and contribute to the preservation of our planet.

Through examples and personal anecdotes, we illustrate how minimalism can create a sense of fulfillment by allowing us to prioritize experiences, relationships, and personal growth over material possessions. By simplifying our lives, we open up opportunities for meaningful connections, personal development, and pursuing our passions.

It is important to note that embracing minimalism is a journey, and sustaining a minimalist lifestyle requires ongoing commitment and self-reflection. We provide practical tips and guidance on how to maintain a minimalist mindset in the long term, including strategies for dealing with external pressures and societal expectations around consumption.

By incorporating minimalism into our lives, we can experience the numerous benefits it offers, from increased mental clarity and reduced stress to a deeper sense of contentment and fulfillment. Embracing minimalism allows us to create a space for what truly matters and live a more intentional, purposeful life.

Understanding Clutter:

In this section, we delve into the detrimental effects of clutter on both our physical and mental well-being. By exploring the underlying psychological reasons behind our tendency to accumulate material possessions, we gain valuable insights into the roots of clutter in our lives. Additionally, we identify and examine different types of clutter that may be present, ranging from physical clutter in our living spaces to digital clutter on our devices and even emotional clutter within ourselves.

The negative impacts of clutter on our physical health cannot be understated. The accumulation of possessions can lead to a cluttered and disorganized living environment, making it difficult to navigate and find what we need. This can result in increased stress levels and even pose safety hazards in extreme cases. Furthermore, excessive clutter can contribute to poor indoor air quality, as dust and allergens tend to accumulate more readily in crowded spaces.

On a psychological level, clutter can have a profound impact on our mental well-being. A cluttered environment often reflects a cluttered mind, leading to feelings of overwhelm, anxiety, and discontentment. It can impede our ability to focus and concentrate, making it challenging to accomplish tasks efficiently. Moreover, studies have shown a correlation between high levels of clutter and increased levels of cortisol, the stress hormone.

Understanding the psychological factors that contribute to clutter is essential in addressing and overcoming this issue. Our attachment to material possessions often stems from emotional connections, sentimental value, or the fear of letting go. By exploring these underlying reasons, we can begin to separate our sense of self-worth from our belongings and develop healthier relationships with our possessions.

Different types of clutter require specific attention and strategies for decluttering. Physical clutter refers to the accumulation of tangible items that take up space in our homes or work environments. This could range from clothes and furniture to kitchen gadgets and personal mementos. Digital clutter, on the other hand, encompasses the overwhelming number of files, emails, and apps that clutter our devices and online spaces. Finally, emotional clutter relates to unresolved emotions, negative thought patterns, and mental baggage that can weigh us down and prevent personal growth.

By understanding the negative consequences of clutter and identifying its various forms, we can begin to take proactive steps towards decluttering and simplifying our lives. Through intentional decision-making, letting go of unnecessary possessions, and creating organized systems for our belongings, we pave the way for a more uncluttered and fulfilling existence.

Practical Tips for Decluttering:

1. Assessing and prioritizing belongings: Begin the decluttering process by assessing each item in your living space. Ask yourself if it serves a purpose, brings you joy, or has practical value. Prioritize items that hold special sentimental value or are essential for daily use.

2. Letting go of unnecessary items: Overcoming emotional attachment to possessions can be challenging but is crucial for effective decluttering. Adopt a mindset that focuses on the benefits of letting go, such as creating more physical and mental space, reducing maintenance and cleaning tasks, and allowing room for new opportunities and experiences.

3. Utilize clutter elimination techniques: To avoid feeling overwhelmed, break the decluttering process into manageable tasks. Consider using methods like the Four-Box Method (sorting items into categories of Keep, Donate/Sell, Trash, and Unsure), the KonMari Method (evaluating items based on whether they spark joy), or the one-in-one-out rule (for every new item brought in, get rid of an equivalent item).

4. Organizing and categorizing belongings: Once you have decluttered, maximize space and functionality by organizing remaining items. Utilize storage solutions such as bins, baskets, shelves, and drawer dividers to neatly categorize belongings. Group similar items together, ensuring easy access and efficient

use of space.

5. Implement a sustainable system: To maintain a clutter-free environment, establish habits and routines that promote tidiness and prevent accumulation of unnecessary items. Regularly reassess your possessions to weed out any new clutter that may have accumulated over time. Consider adopting a minimalist mindset when shopping, focusing on quality rather than quantity and prioritizing needs over wants.

Remember, decluttering is not about getting rid of everything you own but rather creating a living space that aligns with your values and promotes a more fulfilled life. By embracing minimalism and simplifying your surroundings, you can experience the benefits of reduced stress, improved focus, and a greater sense of contentment.

Simplifying Daily Life:

In this section, we explore the importance of simplifying daily routines and commitments to reduce overwhelm and increase productivity, ultimately leading to a more fulfilled life. We provide practical tips and strategies for streamlining household tasks, such as meal planning, cleaning, and organizing.

One of the fundamental principles of minimalism is to eliminate unnecessary complexities in our lives. By simplifying our daily routines, we free up time and mental energy for activities that truly matter to us. We discuss the concept of "decision fatigue" and how reducing the number of choices we have to make throughout the day can lead to increased focus and productivity.

Meal planning is a key aspect of simplifying daily life. We share practical tips on how to plan meals in advance, create grocery lists, and minimize food waste. By having a clear idea of what we will be cooking and eating each day, we can save time, money, and reduce stress associated with last-minute meal decisions.

Cleaning and organizing our living spaces is another essential aspect of simplification. We delve into effective decluttering techniques that help create a clutter-free environment conducive to peace and clarity. From establishing a system for regularly tidying up to designating specific storage spaces for different items, we offer guidance on creating an organized living space that promotes ease and simplicity.

Moreover, we understand that achieving a simplified life goes beyond physical tasks. We address the importance of freeing ourselves from commitments that do not align with our values or bring us joy. By prioritizing activities that truly matter to us and learning to say no to unnecessary obligations, we create more time and space for the things that bring us fulfillment. We guide readers on how to identify their core values and align their daily schedules accordingly, fostering a sense of purpose and satisfaction.

As readers navigate through this chapter, they will gain valuable insights on simplifying daily life from a minimalistic perspective. Whether it's through meal planning, cleaning and organizing, or aligning commitments with personal values, embracing minimalism offers a pathway to a more fulfilled life.

Sustaining a Minimalist Lifestyle:

Maintaining a minimalist mindset in the long term is essential for experiencing the full benefits of a simplified and clutter-free life. While decluttering and simplifying initially may feel liberating, it's important to develop strategies to sustain this lifestyle over time. Here are some effective tips for maintaining a minimalist lifestyle:

1. Embrace intentional consumption: Avoid falling into the trap of mindless consumerism by adopting a mindful approach to your purchases. Before buying something, ask yourself if it aligns

with your values and if it truly adds value to your life. By being intentional about what you bring into your home, you can prevent unnecessary clutter from accumulating.

2. Practice gratitude: Cultivating a sense of gratitude can help reinforce your minimalist mindset. Regularly take time to appreciate the belongings you have and the freedom that comes with a clutter-free space. When you recognize the abundance in your life, it becomes easier to resist the urge to accumulate more possessions.

3. Set boundaries and limits: Establish clear boundaries for what you allow into your living space. This can include implementing a one-in-one-out policy, where for every new item you bring in, you let go of an existing one. Additionally, consider setting guidelines for what type of gifts or items you will accept from others, ensuring they align with your minimalistic values.

4. Surround yourself with inspiration: Create an environment that supports your minimalistic lifestyle by surrounding yourself with visual reminders of why you chose this path. Display inspirational quotes, meaningful artwork, or images that inspire simplicity and contentment. Surrounding yourself with these reminders can help reinforce your commitment to minimalism.

5. Find support and community: Seek out like-minded individuals who share your interest in minimalism. Join online communities or attend local meetups and events where you can connect with others on the same journey. Sharing experiences, advice, and challenges with others can provide valuable support and motivation to stay on track.

6. Regularly declutter and reassess: Avoid complacency by regularly evaluating your belongings and reassessing their value in your life. Create a routine for decluttering specific areas of your home periodically to prevent clutter from accumulating again. By continuously evaluating your possessions, you can ensure that they continue to align with your goals, values, and vision for a

fulfilled life.

Remember, maintaining a minimalist lifestyle is an ongoing process. It requires consistent effort and self-reflection to resist the allure of consumerism and external pressures. However, by staying committed to the principles of minimalism and finding joy in simplicity, you can experience lasting fulfillment and contentment in all aspects of your life.

MOTTAINAI AND SOCIAL RESPONSIBILITY: CREATING POSITIVE CHANGE IN COMMUNITIES

In this chapter, we explore the powerful connection between Mottainai and social responsibility, shedding light on how embracing Mottainai principles can create positive change within communities. Mottainai, with its profound emphasis on regret over waste and mindful resource utilization, serves as a catalyst for fostering a sense of social responsibility and community engagement.

At its core, Mottainai encourages individuals to recognize their interconnectedness with others and the world around them. By cultivating an awareness of the impact of our actions and consumption habits, we can begin to realize the importance of collective action in creating a better future for all.

Mottainai teaches us that every small action matters, and by embodying its principles, we become agents of change within our communities. It prompts us to consider not only our own well-being and prosperity but also the well-being of those around us. Through this mindset shift, we recognize that our individual choices have ripple effects that extend far beyond ourselves.

As we embark on this exploration of Mottainai's role in social responsibility, we will delve into inspiring examples of successful initiatives and organizations that have embraced Mottainai principles. We will examine their strategies, impact, and the challenges they have faced, offering valuable insights into how similar endeavors can be replicated or adapted to suit different community settings.

This chapter aims to inspire readers to take an active role in creating positive change within their own communities through Mottainai-inspired projects. We will provide practical tips and guidelines for individuals and groups looking to initiate such projects, emphasizing the importance of collaboration, resource sharing, and education within communities.

By highlighting the transformative power of Mottainai in promoting a sense of responsibility, empowerment, and unity within communities, we hope to ignite a collective spirit that motivates people to come together and address pressing environmental and social issues. By working collectively towards common goals, we can amplify the impact of Mottainai at a global scale and contribute to broader movements for sustainability and social justice.

As we delve into the examples, strategies, and inspiring stories within this chapter, let us remember that each of us has the power to make a difference. By embracing Mottainai and integrating its principles into our communities, we can create lasting positive change that reverberates far beyond our individual actions. Let us embark on this journey towards social responsibility together, united by the vision of a more sustainable, equitable, and harmonious world.

Examples of Successful Mottainai Initiatives in Communities

Throughout the world, there are numerous organizations and initiatives that have wholeheartedly embraced Mottainai principles to create positive change in their communities. These inspiring examples serve as beacons of hope, demonstrating the power of collective action and the profound impact that can be achieved through mindful resource utilization and social responsibility.

One notable initiative is the Zero Waste Village Project in Kamikatsu, Japan. This small rural community made a commitment to achieve zero waste by 2020, an ambitious goal that required the active participation of every resident. Through extensive recycling programs, composting, and education campaigns, Kamikatsu has successfully reduced its waste output to almost zero. Their groundbreaking efforts have garnered international attention and inspired other communities around the globe to follow suit.

In Singapore, the Sustainable Singapore Blueprint was launched in 2015 with the aim of transforming the city-state into a sustainable and liveable environment for its residents. The blueprint focuses on various aspects of sustainability, including waste reduction and recycling. By implementing innovative waste management strategies such as mandatory recycling programs, promoting eco-packaging, and encouraging businesses to adopt sustainable practices, Singapore has made significant progress towards achieving its vision of becoming a "zero-waste nation."

Another inspiring example comes from California, where the city of San Francisco has implemented comprehensive policies and programs to promote recycling and composting. Through a combination of strict regulations, community engagement initiatives, and public education campaigns, San Francisco has diverted over 80% of its waste away from landfills. The city's success not only benefits the environment but also contributes to job creation and economic growth within the recycling and composting sectors.

In addition to these municipal initiatives, there are numerous grassroots organizations that have taken up the mantle of Mottainai principles. One such organization is Food Rescue US, which operates across several cities in the United States. Their dedicated volunteers work tirelessly to collect excess fresh food from restaurants, grocery stores, and events and redistribute it to local shelters and community programs. By rescuing food that would otherwise go to waste, Food Rescue US not only addresses hunger but also reduces landfill waste and the associated environmental impacts.

While these examples showcase the power of Mottainai principles in creating positive change, it is important to acknowledge the challenges faced by these initiatives. Obstacles such as limited resources, resistance to change, and lack of awareness can pose significant hurdles. However, through determination, collaboration, and creative problem-solving, these organizations have overcome obstacles and continue to make a tangible difference in their communities.

These successful Mottainai initiatives serve as role models for communities worldwide, demonstrating the transformative potential of embracing mindful resource utilization and social responsibility. By learning from their strategies and experiences, individuals and groups can be inspired to take action in their own communities, fostering a sense of unity and empowerment as they work towards a more sustainable and inclusive future.

Strategies for Implementing Mottainai Principles in Community Settings

Implementing Mottainai principles within community settings is a powerful way to create positive change and foster social responsibility. Here, we provide practical tips and guidelines that individuals and groups can use to initiate Mottainai-inspired projects in their communities. By following these strategies, communities can establish a strong foundation for sustainable practices and a collective sense of responsibility.

1. Collaboration and Partnerships:
One of the key aspects of implementing Mottainai principles is collaboration. Seek out like-minded individuals, organizations, and businesses within your community who share a passion for sustainability and waste reduction. By establishing partnerships and working together, you can leverage each other's strengths, resources, and expertise to achieve common goals. Collaborative efforts not only maximize impact but also build a sense of shared responsibility and unity within the community.

2. Resource Sharing:
Embracing resource sharing is a fundamental principle of Mottainai. Encourage community members to share tools, equipment, and other resources that are not regularly used, eliminating the need for unnecessary duplication. Establish platforms or networks where community members can easily borrow or lend items, fostering a culture of convenience, efficiency, and mindful consumption. This not only reduces waste but also cultivates a spirit of communal support and interconnectedness.

3. Education and Awareness:
Education plays a vital role in the implementation of Mottainai principles within communities. Raise awareness about the importance of waste reduction, sustainable living, and mindful consumption through workshops, seminars, educational campaigns, and community events. Share success stories and case studies that showcase the positive impact of Mottainai practices. By educating community members about the benefits and potential solutions, you empower them to make informed choices and actively participate in sustainable initiatives.

4. Local Policy Advocacy:
Advocating for supportive local policies is crucial in making lasting changes at the community level. Engage with local government officials, community leaders, and relevant stakeholders to promote policies that encourage waste reduction, recycling programs, and sustainable practices. By actively participating in policy discussions and decision-making processes, you can create an enabling environment for Mottainai initiatives to thrive.

5. Community-led Projects:
Empower and encourage community members to take the lead in initiating Mottainai-inspired projects. These projects can range from setting up community gardens, organizing clothing swaps, establishing repair cafes or composting centers, to promoting circular economy practices within local businesses. Encourage creativity, innovation, and entrepreneurship within the community by supporting individuals who have ideas for sustainable projects. By nurturing these initiatives, communities can become self-sufficient in addressing their waste management and sustainability needs.

6. Evaluation and Progress Tracking:
Establish a system for evaluating and tracking the progress of Mottainai initiatives within the community. Regularly assess the impact of implemented programs, collect feedback from participants, and identify areas for improvement. This monitoring process helps to identify successful strategies, learn from challenges faced, and adapt approaches as needed. Celebrate achievements and milestones to inspire further engagement and sustain momentum within the community.

By implementing these strategies, communities can create a vibrant ecosystem of Mottainai-inspired practices that foster social responsibility and create lasting positive change. Collaboration, resource sharing, education, advocacy, community-led projects, and evaluation form the foundation upon which communities can build a more sustainable and mindful future together. Embrace these strategies and watch as your community becomes a model for others seeking to transform their wasteful habits into meaningful actions.

Inspiring Community Engagement through Mottainai Principles

Mottainai not only encourages individuals to embrace the concept of 'no waste' in their personal lives but also holds the potential to create a powerful sense of responsibility, empowerment, and unity within communities. By rallying together around the principles of Mottainai, communities can address environmental and social issues, driving positive change on a local level.

One inspiring example of community engagement through Mottainai principles can be found in the small town of Greenville. In an effort to reduce waste and promote sustainability, residents came together to establish a community garden. By sharing resources such as land, tools, and knowledge, they were able to create a thriving space that not only provided fresh produce for the community but also fostered a sense of connection and shared responsibility. Through regular gatherings and workshops, the garden became a hub for education on sustainable practices and a catalyst for positive change.

Similarly, in the urban neighborhood of Harmony Heights, residents organized a community-wide swap meet. This event encouraged neighbors to bring unwanted items from their homes and exchange them for something they needed. The swap meet not only reduced waste by giving new life to gently used items but also built a sense of camaraderie among residents. The event sparked conversations about mindful consumption and resource sharing, leading to lasting changes in individual shopping habits.

In both these examples, Mottainai principles played a pivotal role in fostering community engagement. By emphasizing the shared responsibility towards our environment and resources, individuals were inspired to take action and collaborate towards a common goal. These initiatives underscored the power of collective effort and demonstrated how small actions taken together can have a significant impact.

To inspire community engagement through Mottainai principles, it is essential to provide educational opportunities. Workshops and seminars focused on sustainable living practices can help raise awareness and empower individuals with the knowledge needed to make informed choices. By organizing events like clean-up drives, recycling initiatives, or community-based projects that repurpose waste materials, communities can strengthen their sense of responsibility and promote a culture of sustainability.

Communication and collaboration are key to building community engagement. Platforms such as community social media groups or neighborhood newsletters can be used to share success stories, tips, and ideas for embracing Mottainai principles. By fostering open dialogue and encouraging participation, communities can create a supportive environment that nurtures the value of mindful consumption and waste reduction.

The impact of community engagement through Mottainai principles does not stop at the local level but has the potential to ripple out on a global scale. By sharing their successes and lessons learned, communities can inspire others around the world to adopt similar practices. Social media platforms, online forums, and networking events can serve as powerful avenues for connecting communities and amplifying the impact of Mottainai initiatives.

In conclusion, Mottainai principles have the power to inspire community engagement by promoting a sense of responsibility, empowerment, and unity. By sharing success stories and fostering open communication, communities can come together to address environmental and social issues, leading to positive change both locally and globally. Embracing Mottainai within communities is not only an act of sustainability but also a testament to the transformative power of collective action.

The Ripple Effect: Amplifying Mottainai's Impact at a Global Scale

As we have explored in previous chapters, Mottainai holds immense potential for creating positive change within communities. The principles of Mottainai, such as resource sharing, responsible consumption, and waste reduction, can foster a sense of social responsibility and empowerment among individuals. However, the impact of Mottainai extends far beyond the boundaries of individual communities. In this final section of the chapter on Mottainai and Social Responsibility, we will delve into how local Mottainai initiatives have the power to amplify their impact on a global scale.

Local Mottainai initiatives serve as catalysts for broader global movements. By implementing Mottainai principles within their communities, individuals and organizations create tangible examples of sustainable practices that inspire others around the world. These initiatives showcase the potential of Mottainai to address pressing environmental and social challenges, encouraging others to adopt similar approaches.

One way that local Mottainai efforts can expand their impact globally is by leveraging technology and digital platforms. In today's interconnected world, it has become easier than ever to share knowledge, ideas, and success stories across borders. Local Mottainai projects can utilize social media, online forums, and virtual networks to reach a wider audience and inspire people from diverse backgrounds to embrace Mottainai principles.

Collaboration across borders is another powerful way to amplify the impact of Mottainai. By connecting with like-minded individuals and organizations around the world, local Mottainai initiatives can tap into a global network of resources, expertise, and support. Collaborative efforts enable communities to learn from each other's experiences, leverage shared knowledge and best practices, and collectively work towards common goals.

Furthermore, engaging in international platforms and conferences can provide opportunities for local Mottainai projects to share their achievements, challenges, and lessons learned with a global audience. By actively participating in these events, communities can contribute to shaping the broader discourse on sustainability, waste reduction, and social responsibility. Their experiences provide valuable insights that can inform policies, drive innovation, and inspire collective action on a global scale.

The ripple effect of local Mottainai initiatives can extend far beyond the initial community. By demonstrating the effectiveness of Mottainai principles, these projects inspire individuals, organizations, and governments around the world to adopt similar practices. This not only contributes to a more sustainable and responsible approach to resource utilization but also creates an interconnected network of change-makers who are collectively working towards a common vision.

In conclusion, local Mottainai initiatives have the potential to create a ripple effect that amplifies their impact at a global scale. By utilizing technology, collaborating across borders, and actively engaging in international platforms, local Mottainai projects can inspire others and contribute to broader movements focused on sustainability, waste reduction, and social responsibility. As we continue our journey towards a happier, richer, and more fulfilled life through embracing Mottainai, let us remember the power we hold as individuals and communities to make a positive difference in the world.

NURTURING RELATIONSHIPS THROUGH SHARED RESOURCES: THE POWER OF COMMUNITY SHARING

Community sharing is a powerful manifestation of the Mottainai principles, emphasizing the efficient and collaborative use of resources. It involves individuals coming together to share items, spaces, or skills, fostering relationships built on trust, cooperation, and mutual support. Community sharing initiatives are rooted in the understanding that by pooling our resources and reducing consumption, we can create sustainable and thriving communities.

Connection to Mottainai Principles:
Community sharing aligns perfectly with the core tenets of Mottainai - appreciating the value of resources, minimizing waste, and nurturing a sense of responsibility for the well-being of our communities and the planet. By embracing community sharing, we embrace the idea that there is abundance in what we already have, and by working together, we can make the most out of our

collective resources.

Fostering Relationships and Collaboration:

Community sharing not only facilitates resource optimization but also fosters deeper connections and collaborations within communities. When individuals come together to share their possessions or skills, they build trust and forge meaningful relationships. Through shared experiences, people learn from one another, support each other's needs, and create a strong sense of belonging. The act of sharing in itself becomes a catalyst for social cohesion and community empowerment.

Optimizing Resource Utilization:

By sharing resources, communities can significantly reduce waste and minimize their environmental footprint. For instance, a tool library allows members to borrow tools they may need for a specific project without having to purchase them individually. This not only saves money for individuals but also reduces the manufacturing demand for new tools. Similarly, community gardens provide an opportunity for neighbors to grow their own food collectively, ensuring that land and resources are utilized efficiently.

Promoting Sustainable Living Practices:

Community sharing initiatives inspire sustainable living practices by encouraging individuals to be mindful consumers and considerate sharers. When resources are shared, there is a natural inclination to use them responsibly and take care of them for the benefit of the entire community. By embracing community sharing, we foster an ethos of sustainability, where waste is minimized, and appreciation for the value of resources is ingrained in our daily lives.

In the following sections, we will explore different types of community sharing initiatives, discuss their benefits, and provide guidance on how to start and sustain these initiatives in your own communities. We will also share inspiring success stories from around the world that demonstrate the transformative power of community sharing. Together, let us discover how the act of sharing can not only optimize resource utilization but also nurture relationships and empower communities.

Types of Community Sharing Initiatives

Community sharing initiatives come in various forms, each with its own unique benefits and contributions to fostering a sense of Mottainai within a community. Here, we explore some of the most common types of community sharing initiatives that have gained popularity around the world.

1. Tool Libraries:
Tool libraries provide community members with access to a wide range of tools and equipment that they may need for various projects and repairs. From power tools to gardening equipment, tool libraries allow individuals to borrow items on a temporary basis, reducing the need for each household to purchase and store their own tools. This not only saves money but also promotes sustainable resource utilization and encourages collaborative problem-solving within the community.

2. Toy Libraries:
Toy libraries are an excellent way to promote Mottainai principles while providing children with access to a diverse array of toys and games. These libraries allow parents or caregivers to borrow toys for a specific period, ensuring that children can experience a variety of playthings without contributing to excessive waste or clutter. By sharing toys, communities can reduce the environmental impact of toy production and disposal while fostering a culture of reuse and resourcefulness among children.

3. Community Gardens:
Community gardens bring neighbors together by transforming unused or underutilized spaces into vibrant green areas for growing fruits, vegetables, herbs, and flowers. By sharing

land, seeds, tools, and knowledge, community members can collectively cultivate fresh produce while building relationships and fostering a sense of stewardship towards the earth. Community gardens not only promote sustainable food production but also contribute to food security, education, and overall well-being.

4. Car-Sharing Programs:

Car-sharing programs provide an alternative to individual car ownership by allowing community members to share vehicles for their transportation needs. By utilizing shared cars instead of owning personal vehicles, participants can reduce fuel consumption, traffic congestion, and carbon emissions. Car-sharing initiatives often involve flexible booking systems and affordable rates, making it a convenient and cost-effective solution for those who do not require a car on a daily basis.

5. Community Kitchens:

Community kitchens are communal spaces where individuals can come together to prepare and share meals. These initiatives encourage collaboration, social interaction, and the sharing of culinary knowledge. By pooling resources and cooking collectively, community members can reduce food waste, share the workload, and foster a strong sense of unity within the community. Community kitchens often organize events and workshops centered around sustainable cooking practices and the use of locally sourced ingredients.

These examples represent just a fraction of the diverse community sharing initiatives that exist worldwide. Each initiative embodies the spirit of Mottainai by encouraging resource optimization, collaboration, and the reduction of waste. By participating in these initiatives, communities not only minimize their environmental impact but also nurture stronger relationships, support local economies, and create spaces where everyone can thrive together.

Benefits of Community Sharing

Community sharing initiatives offer a wide range of social, economic, and environmental benefits that contribute to a more sustainable and interconnected society. By fostering a sense of collaboration, trust, and resource optimization, community sharing not only strengthens communities but also reduces waste and promotes responsible consumption. In this section, we explore in depth the numerous advantages of embracing community sharing practices.

Social Benefits:

1. Building Trust and Strengthening Relationships: Community sharing encourages individuals to connect with their neighbors and build relationships based on trust and mutual support. Through shared resources and collaborative efforts, people develop a sense of belonging and camaraderie within their communities.

2. Enhancing Social Cohesion: Sharing resources fosters a culture of reciprocity and collective responsibility. By engaging in community sharing initiatives, individuals feel a stronger bond with their neighbors and develop a deeper sense of community spirit.

3. Empowering Individuals: Community sharing empowers individuals by providing them access to resources they may not have otherwise been able to afford or obtain. This inclusivity promotes equality and enables individuals to enhance their quality of life without placing excessive strain on their finances.

Economic Benefits:

1. Cost Savings: Participating in community sharing initiatives allows individuals to save money by accessing shared resources rather than purchasing or owning items individually. Whether

it's borrowing tools from a tool library or sharing a car through a car-sharing program, community sharing offers cost-effective alternatives to traditional ownership.

2. Resource Optimization: Community sharing optimizes the utilization of existing resources, resulting in more efficient distribution and reduced waste. By maximizing the use of shared resources, communities can minimize overconsumption and contribute to a more sustainable economy.

3. Economic Resilience: Community sharing initiatives foster local economies by promoting local businesses and reducing reliance on large corporations. When individuals support local sharing initiatives, they help stimulate economic growth within their own communities.

Environmental Benefits:

1. Waste Reduction: Community sharing initiatives play a significant role in reducing waste by promoting the reuse and repurposing of resources. By sharing items instead of discarding them, communities can minimize their impact on landfills and contribute to a circular economy.

2. Sustainable Consumption: Community sharing encourages responsible consumption by shifting the focus from individual ownership to shared access. This shift in mindset promotes mindful resource utilization, reducing the demand for new products and minimizing environmental degradation.

3. Conservation of Natural Resources: Sharing resources reduces the need for excessive extraction of natural resources. By maximizing the lifespan and utility of existing resources, community sharing initiatives contribute to the preservation of our planet's finite resources.

In conclusion, community sharing initiatives offer numerous social, economic, and environmental benefits that contribute to a more sustainable and fulfilling way of life. These initiatives build trust, strengthen relationships, reduce waste, save money, and promote responsible consumption practices. By embracing community sharing, individuals can actively participate in creating a more interconnected and resilient society.

How to Start a Community Sharing Initiative

Starting a community sharing initiative is an exciting and rewarding endeavor that can bring people together, foster a sense of belonging, and create positive change in your neighborhood or community. Here is a step-by-step guide on how to establish a successful community sharing initiative:

1. Identify the needs and interests of your community: Begin by understanding the specific needs and interests of your community. Conduct surveys or host community meetings to gather information about the resources that community members may be willing to share or access through sharing.

2. Form a core group of enthusiastic individuals: Find like-minded individuals who are passionate about community sharing and willing to dedicate time and effort to make the initiative a reality. This core group will serve as the driving force behind the project and help establish guidelines and logistics.

3. Research existing models and learn from success stories: Look for existing community sharing initiatives in other areas or online platforms that promote resource sharing. Study their models, understand their successes and challenges, and adapt their best practices to fit the unique needs of your community.

4. Determine the scope and focus of your initiative: Decide on the scope and focus of your community sharing initiative. Will it be centered around tools and equipment, books and media, gardening resources, or something else? Define the specific areas you will target to ensure clarity and effectiveness.

5. Establish guidelines and protocols: Create clear guidelines and

protocols that outline how the sharing initiative will operate. Consider factors such as membership requirements, borrowing periods, maintenance responsibilities, and liability issues. Collaborate with legal experts if necessary to ensure the initiative is set up in compliance with local laws and regulations.

6. Identify potential partners and collaborators: Reach out to local businesses, organizations, schools, and community centers that may be interested in participating or supporting your initiative. These partnerships can provide valuable resources, spaces for storage or meetings, and help spread awareness about the initiative.

7. Develop a system for communication and coordination: Establish effective communication channels to keep participants informed about available resources, upcoming events, and updates on the initiative. Utilize online platforms, social media, newsletters, or community notice boards to ensure transparent and consistent communication.

8. Create a physical or virtual space for sharing: Depending on the nature of your initiative, set up a physical space where community members can borrow or access shared resources. Alternatively, create a virtual platform or online database where members can list and request items for borrowing or sharing.

9. Organize events and workshops: Arrange regular events and workshops that promote the sharing culture within your community. These could include skill-sharing sessions, repair cafes, or resource exchange fairs, where community members can come together to learn, share, and connect.

10. Promote participation and inclusivity: Develop strategies to encourage active participation from diverse members of the community. Consider organizing outreach programs, offering incentives for involvement, or creating educational campaigns that highlight the importance of community sharing and its benefits.

11. Evaluate and adapt: Continuously assess the effectiveness of your community sharing initiative by gauging participation levels, obtaining feedback from community members, and monitoring its impact. Adapt and modify your model as needed to address challenges and better meet the evolving needs of your community.

By following these steps, you can lay a strong foundation for a thriving community sharing initiative that fosters relationships, amplifies resource utilization, and brings sustainable living practices to life in your community. Remember, even small efforts can make a significant difference when it comes to nurturing relationships through shared resources.

Success Stories in Community Sharing

1. The Tool Library: A Beacon of Collaboration and Resourcefulness
- Profile of a successful tool library in a small community
- Description of how the tool library operates, lending tools to community members for various projects
- Discussion on its impact in fostering collaboration, building relationships, and reducing unnecessary tool purchases

2. The Toy Library: Building Stronger Ties Among Families
- Showcase of a thriving toy library that provides access to a wide range of toys for families with young children
- Explanation of how the toy library promotes play, socialization, and reduces toy waste
- Testimonials from parents about the positive influence of the toy library on their children's development and family bonds

3. Community Gardens: Cultivating Connections and Sustainable Food Practices
- Examination of the benefits of community gardens in urban environments

- Case study showcasing a successful community garden that brings together diverse individuals and fosters food security
- Analysis of the positive impact on participants' well-being, social connections, and sustainable food practices

4. Car-Sharing Programs: Reducing Traffic Congestion and Carbon Emissions
- Overview of car-sharing programs as a solution to transportation challenges in densely populated areas
- Success story of a car-sharing initiative that has significantly reduced private car ownership and increased access to affordable transportation options
- Evaluation of the program's impact on reducing traffic congestion, carbon emissions, and improving air quality

5. Neighborhood Tool Sharing: Strengthening Bonds and Expanding Skillsets
- Exploration of neighborhood-based tool sharing initiatives, where neighbors share tools and expertise
- Real-life examples highlighting the benefits of such initiatives, including cost savings, increased self-sufficiency, and strengthened community ties
- Discussion on how these initiatives empower individuals to develop new skills and pursue DIY projects with confidence

These success stories serve as an inspiration for readers to understand the transformative power of community sharing initiatives. By showcasing real-life examples of how these initiatives have made a positive impact on community cohesion, resource utilization, and sustainable living practices, readers are encouraged to envision the potential within their own neighborhoods or communities. Through the power of community sharing, individuals can nurture relationships, promote collaboration, and contribute to a more sustainable and fulfilling way of life.

MOTTAINAI IN EDUCATION: INSTILLING VALUES OF CONSERVATION AND SUSTAINABILITY IN THE NEXT GENERATION

Education plays a crucial role in shaping the values and attitudes of the next generation. It provides an avenue for promoting conservation and sustainability, making it essential to integrate Mottainai principles into educational curricula.

Mottainai offers a unique perspective on waste and resource utilization, emphasizing the importance of minimizing waste and appreciating the value of resources. By incorporating Mottainai principles into education, we can instill a sense of responsibility and mindfulness in students from an early age.

Schools have the power to shape students' attitudes towards waste and resource utilization. By teaching Mottainai principles, educators can help students understand the environmental impact of their actions and make informed choices to reduce waste. They can also cultivate a deeper appreciation for resources, fostering a mindset that values durability and long-term sustainability.

Integrating Mottainai into educational curricula can take various forms. For example, it can be incorporated into science lessons, where students learn about ecosystems and their delicate balance. By highlighting how wasting resources disrupts this balance, students can develop a greater understanding of the significance of conservation.

Mottainai can also be integrated into economics and mathematics lessons, where students can learn about the economic implications of wasteful practices. By exploring concepts such as cost-benefit analysis and sustainable consumption patterns, students can gain practical skills in decision-making that align with Mottainai principles.

Furthermore, arts and crafts classes provide opportunities for creativity and upcycling. Students can learn to repurpose materials and create new items from what would have otherwise been discarded. This not only promotes resourcefulness but also reinforces the concept of transforming waste into something valuable.

To effectively teach Mottainai in schools, educators need to be equipped with the necessary materials and resources. This includes access to up-to-date information on sustainable practices, lesson plans specifically designed around Mottainai principles, and support from relevant organizations or agencies.

While integrating Mottainai into education can bring about positive change, there may be challenges along the way. Resistance from traditional teaching methods or limited resources could hinder the implementation process. However, by highlighting the benefits of Mottainai education and fostering collaboration among teachers, parents, and the wider community, these obstacles can be overcome.

In conclusion, integrating Mottainai principles into educational curricula is crucial for instilling values of conservation and sustainability in the next generation. Schools play a significant role in shaping students' attitudes towards waste and resource utilization, making it essential to embrace Mottainai as a guiding principle. By incorporating Mottainai into various subjects and grade levels, educators can empower students to become responsible stewards of the environment and catalysts for positive change.

Examples of Programs and Schools Incorporating Sustainability Education and Waste Reduction Practices:

1. Green Schools Initiative: The Green Schools Initiative is a nonprofit organization that works with schools to create sustainable environments and empower students to become environmental stewards. Through their comprehensive programs, schools are encouraged to adopt waste reduction practices such as composting, recycling, and implementing zero-waste initiatives. Profiles of schools that have successfully implemented the Green Schools Initiative will be showcased, highlighting their waste reduction efforts and the positive impact on both the school community and the environment.

2. Sustainable Schools Network: The Sustainable Schools Network is a global network of schools that aims to promote sustainability education and practices. This network provides resources, training, and support to schools looking to incorporate sustainability into their curriculum and operations. Examples of schools within the network will be featured, showcasing their innovative approaches to waste reduction, energy conservation, and promoting sustainable lifestyles. These case studies will highlight the various strategies employed by schools to engage students in hands-on learning experiences that foster a sense of responsibility towards waste reduction.

3. Eco-Schools Program: The Eco-Schools Program is an internationally recognized program that empowers students to drive sustainable change within their school communities. Participating schools undertake a holistic approach to sustainability, addressing various environmental pillars including waste management, energy conservation, water efficiency, and biodiversity preservation. By exploring successful Eco-Schools projects from around the world, readers will gain insights into the practical implementation of Mottainai principles within educational settings. These examples will demonstrate how student-led initiatives can effectively reduce waste and inspire positive behavior change among peers.

4. Outdoor Learning Initiatives: Numerous schools have embraced outdoor learning initiatives as a means to connect students with nature while instilling values of conservation and sustainability. Through outdoor classrooms, eco-gardens, and nature-based activities, these schools provide students with opportunities to learn about ecosystems, natural resource management, and waste reduction practices. Real-life examples of outdoor learning programs will be highlighted, emphasizing their impact on students' understanding of Mottainai and their commitment to responsible resource consumption.

5. Waste Reduction Campaigns: Many schools have created waste reduction campaigns that actively involve students in the process of minimizing waste generation. These campaigns often include recycling drives, awareness campaigns, and creative projects using recycled materials. Case studies of successful waste reduction campaigns will be shared, showcasing how schools effectively engage students, teachers, and the wider community in embracing Mottainai principles. These examples will highlight the creativity and ingenuity displayed by students in finding innovative solutions to waste reduction challenges.

Through the exploration of these programs and schools, readers will gain a deeper understanding of how Mottainai principles can be integrated into educational settings. The profiles presented will inspire educators, administrators, and parents to support and advocate for sustainability education, leading to a generation of environmentally conscious individuals who understand the importance of waste reduction and resource appreciation.

Practical approaches for incorporating Mottainai principles into various subjects and grade levels can provide students with valuable knowledge and skills to become more conscious consumers and caretakers of the environment. Here, we will explore specific strategies for teaching Mottainai in schools, ensuring that this important concept is integrated seamlessly into the curriculum.

1. Cross-Curricular Integration:
One effective way to introduce Mottainai principles is through cross-curricular integration. By weaving Mottainai concepts into multiple subjects, such as science, social studies, language arts, and even math, students can develop a holistic understanding of waste reduction, sustainability, and mindful consumption. For example, in science classes, students can learn about natural resources, their extraction processes, and the importance of conservation. In language arts classes, they can explore literature that promotes sustainable living and discuss the ethical implications of waste generation. By approaching Mottainai from different angles, students gain a comprehensive perspective on its relevance in various aspects of life.

2. Project-Based Learning:
Engaging students in project-based learning can be an effective method for teaching Mottainai principles while empowering them to take ownership of their education. Students can work on projects that involve conducting waste audits in their schools or communities, designing eco-friendly products or solutions, or creating campaigns to raise awareness about Mottainai practices.

Through these hands-on experiences, students not only deepen their understanding of Mottainai but also develop critical thinking skills, problem-solving abilities, and a sense of agency in making positive changes.

3. Environmental Education Programs:
Collaborating with environmental education programs and organizations can enhance the teaching of Mottainai principles. These programs often offer workshops, field trips, and resources that align with Mottainai values. By participating in such programs, students can engage in experiential learning opportunities that provide them with real-world examples of sustainable practices. Additionally, inviting environmental experts or guest speakers to share their experiences and knowledge can further enrich students' understanding of Mottainai and inspire them to take action.

4. Infusing Mottainai in School Policies and Practices:
Integrating Mottainai principles into school policies and practices can reinforce the importance of waste reduction and sustainable living. Schools can establish recycling programs, composting initiatives, or zero-waste lunch policies, encouraging students to actively participate in these efforts. By making Mottainai a visible part of the school environment, students are more likely to internalize its principles and incorporate them into their daily lives.

5. Leveraging Technology and Media:
Utilizing technology and media can provide innovative ways to teach Mottainai in schools. Teachers can incorporate videos, documentaries, or interactive online resources that highlight the impact of waste and the benefits of mindful resource utilization. Virtual field trips or video conferences with experts from around the world can expose students to diverse perspectives on Mottainai practices. Similarly, using educational apps or online platforms that promote sustainability education and gamify waste reduction can make learning about Mottainai engaging and

interactive.

Despite the potential challenges of integrating Mottainai into the curriculum, such as time constraints or resistance to change, it is essential to persevere. By equipping students with the knowledge, skills, and values associated with Mottainai, we empower them to become environmentally conscious individuals who contribute positively to society. Through these strategies, educators can cultivate a generation that embraces Mottainai for a happier, richer, and more fulfilled future.

Fostering environmental stewardship and responsibility in students is a crucial aspect of Mottainai education. By instilling the values of conservation and sustainability from a young age, we can empower future generations to take meaningful actions towards creating a more sustainable world.

Mottainai education goes beyond simply teaching students about waste reduction and resource conservation; it aims to cultivate a deep sense of environmental stewardship and responsibility. By understanding the interconnectedness of all living beings and recognizing the impact of our actions on the environment, students can develop a strong sense of responsibility towards preserving and protecting our planet.

Through Mottainai education, students learn to appreciate the value of resources and understand that wastefulness not only harms the environment but also compromises their own future. They become aware of the finite nature of resources and recognize the need for sustainable practices to ensure their availability for future generations.

By engaging students in hands-on activities and practical projects focused on waste reduction, recycling, and sustainable living, Mottainai education encourages them to take ownership of their actions. This active involvement fosters a sense of personal responsibility and empowers students to make informed choices that contribute to a more sustainable future.

Furthermore, the impact of Mottainai education goes beyond the school setting. Students who develop a strong sense of environmental stewardship through Mottainai principles are more likely to translate these values into their daily lives outside of school. They become advocates for change within their families and communities, inspiring others to adopt sustainable practices and reduce waste.

Through Mottainai education, we have the opportunity to shape a generation of environmentally conscious individuals who prioritize sustainability in all facets of life. By instilling values of conservation and sustainability in the next generation, we can create a lasting impact on our planet's future and foster a sense of environmental stewardship that will ripple through society.

Engaging Parents, Teachers, and the Community in Promoting Mottainai Principles

In order to truly instill values of conservation and sustainability in the next generation, it is essential to involve not just students, but also parents, teachers, and the wider community in promoting Mottainai principles. By creating partnerships and fostering collaboration, we can reinforce the importance of waste reduction and mindful resource utilization beyond the classroom.

One effective strategy for engaging parents and caregivers is through educational workshops or seminars. These sessions can provide valuable information on Mottainai principles, explain their significance, and offer practical tips on how families can incorporate these principles into their daily lives. By involving parents in the conversation, we can create a consistent message both at home and at school, reinforcing the importance of Mottainai practices.

Collaboration with teachers is another crucial aspect of

promoting Mottainai principles in education. Educators play a vital role in shaping students' attitudes towards waste and resource utilization. By integrating Mottainai principles into various subjects across different grade levels, teachers can help students understand the impact of waste on the environment and society as a whole. For example, science lessons can focus on the life cycle of products and the consequences of waste accumulation, while art classes can encourage creativity through upcycling projects.

Additionally, involving the wider community in promoting Mottainai principles can have a significant impact. Collaboration with local businesses, organizations, and government agencies can provide opportunities for students to engage in real-world projects that emphasize waste reduction and sustainable practices. For example, students can participate in community clean-up activities or take part in recycling initiatives. By working together with stakeholders outside of the school setting, students gain a broader perspective on the importance of Mottainai principles and their relevance beyond the classroom.

Creating partnerships with community members who share similar values is another effective way to reinforce Mottainai principles. This can involve collaborating with local farmers, artisans, and other individuals or organizations that prioritize sustainability and waste reduction. Students can visit these organizations to gain firsthand experience and learn from their practices. By fostering these connections, we create a network of support that strengthens the message of Mottainai principles throughout the community.

In conclusion, engaging parents, teachers, and the wider community in promoting Mottainai principles is crucial for instilling values of conservation and sustainability in the next generation. Through workshops, collaboration with teachers, involvement from local businesses, and partnerships with community members who share similar values, we can reinforce the importance of Mottainai education both inside and outside the classroom. By working together, we empower students to make a positive impact on the environment and embrace a lifestyle rooted in mindful resource utilization.

Upcycling and Repurposing: Transforming Waste into Works of Art

Upcycling and repurposing are powerful practices that align perfectly with the principles of Mottainai. In this chapter, we explore how waste can be transformed into valuable and functional creations, giving new life to discarded materials and reducing the burden on our environment.

At its core, upcycling involves taking an item that would typically be considered waste and transforming it into something of higher value or quality. This process not only prevents the item from ending up in landfills but also showcases the potential for beauty and usefulness that lies within our discarded possessions. Repurposing, on the other hand, involves finding alternate uses for items that may no longer serve their original purpose.

The act of upcycling and repurposing carries profound significance within the context of Mottainai. By consciously choosing to see value in what others might deem as waste, we embrace a mindset that rejects the culture of disposability that dominates our society. Instead of discarding items without consideration, we strive to extract every ounce of potential from them, turning them into objects that bring joy, functionality, and artistic expression.

More than just a practical approach to waste reduction, upcycling and repurposing become acts of creative rebellion against a throwaway culture. It is a way of asserting our individuality by transforming discarded objects into unique pieces of art. These creations serve as a reminder of the inherent worth in everything around us and reflect our commitment to sustainability and resource conservation.

Furthermore, upcycling and repurposing projects offer endless opportunities for exploration and self-expression. With numerous techniques and methods available, such as furniture restoration, clothing alterations, or transforming household items into decorative pieces, individuals can unleash their creativity and reimagine the potential of discarded materials.

By embracing upcycling and repurposing practices inspired by Mottainai, we can make a tangible impact on both an individual and societal level. Not only do these practices reduce waste and conserve resources, but they also encourage us to question our consumer habits and challenge the notion that new is always better. Through their transformative nature, upcycled and repurposed creations serve as powerful reminders of the incredible potential for change that lies within our own hands.

Throughout the rest of this chapter, we will delve into various techniques and methods used in upcycling, showcase inspiring projects, and highlight artists and businesses that have successfully integrated Mottainai principles into their upcycling practices. Additionally, we will provide readers with practical resources, tools, and tips to embark on their own upcycling and repurposing journey. Together, let us embrace the art of transforming waste into works of art, paving the way for a more sustainable and creative future.

Techniques and Methods for Upcycling:

In the world of upcycling and repurposing, there is an endless array of techniques and methods that can be used to transform waste into stunning works of art. These techniques not only breathe new life into discarded materials but also showcase the immense creativity and ingenuity of artists and craftsmen who embrace the principles of Mottainai.

One popular technique in upcycling is known as "deconstruction."

This involves breaking down an item into its individual components or parts and repurposing them in new ways. For example, an old wooden door could be disassembled and transformed into a unique coffee table by using the panels as the tabletop and the door handles as decorative accents. Deconstruction allows for maximum utilization of all available materials, ensuring minimal waste.

Another technique widely employed in upcycling is "reimagining." This involves viewing ordinary objects in a new light and envisioning alternative uses for them. For instance, empty glass bottles can be turned into stylish vases or candle holders with a coat of paint and some creative embellishments. By reimagining everyday items, artists can create functional yet visually appealing pieces while reducing waste.

One particularly fascinating technique is "collage." This method involves combining various materials, such as fabric scraps, magazine cutouts, or broken ceramics, to create intricate and visually striking compositions. Artists adept at collage can transform seemingly unrelated pieces into cohesive artworks that tell unique stories. The beauty of collage lies in its ability to incorporate even the smallest fragments of waste into something meaningful and beautiful.

Additionally, "upholstery" techniques offer limitless possibilities for transforming old furniture and fabrics. Reupholstering worn-out chairs or sofas with new upholstery fabric breathes new life into them, adding fresh colors and textures that can completely change the look and feel of a space. Upholstery experts employ their skills to repair, restore, and reimagine discarded furniture, ensuring that these pieces continue to be cherished for years to come.

Moreover, "mixed media" techniques enable artists to combine different art forms and materials in their upcycling projects. By merging painting, sculpture, and other artistic disciplines, they can create dynamic and multidimensional artworks that transcend traditional boundaries. For example, an artist could incorporate repurposed metal scraps into a mixed media sculpture, adding texture and visual interest to the piece.

These are just a few of the many techniques and methods used in upcycling and repurposing. The key is to approach the process with an open mind and a willingness to experiment. By learning and mastering various techniques, artists can transform waste materials into extraordinary creations that not only inspire but also contribute to a more sustainable future.

Showcasing the transformative power of upcycling and repurposing, this section highlights a diverse range of creative projects that exemplify the potential of Mottainai-inspired practices. Spanning various art forms, including furniture, fashion, and home decor, these examples inspire readers to see waste materials in a new light and consider the possibilities for their own upcycling endeavors.

One featured project is a stunning coffee table crafted from reclaimed wood and salvaged metal. The artist skillfully combines these discarded materials to create an elegant and functional piece of furniture that adds character and uniqueness to any living space. By embracing Mottainai principles, the artist not only minimizes waste but also elevates discarded materials into true works of art.

In the realm of fashion, a designer presents a collection made entirely from upcycled fabrics and trims. By sourcing materials from thrift stores and textile waste facilities, this visionary designer breathes new life into forgotten garments, creating one-of-a-kind pieces that are both fashionable and sustainable. Through their innovative approach to fashion design, they challenge traditional notions of consumption and demonstrate the power of repurposing in reducing the environmental impact of the fashion industry.

Moving into the domain of home decor, artisans showcase their creativity by transforming discarded glass bottles into exquisite pendant lamps. With meticulous craftsmanship, these artists cut and shape glass bottles into captivating designs that cast intricate patterns of light when illuminated. This upcycling project not only repurposes waste but also adds a touch of artistic elegance to any interior space.

Beyond these specific examples, this section includes a wide array of inspiring upcycling and repurposing projects. From transforming old windows into decorative picture frames to upcycling vintage textiles into statement accessories, each project demonstrates the limitless potential of Mottainai-inspired creativity.

By showcasing these innovative creations, readers gain invaluable inspiration and ideas for their own upcycling and repurposing endeavors. The message is clear: with a little imagination and an embrace of Mottainai principles, waste can be transformed into something remarkable, both functional and beautiful.

Artists and Businesses Embracing Mottainai-Inspired Upcycling:

In this section, we celebrate the creativity and innovation of artists and businesses that have wholeheartedly embraced Mottainai principles in their upcycling practices. These individuals and organizations serve as shining examples of how waste can be transformed into works of art, bringing new life and purpose to discarded materials.

1. Artist Profile: Hiroshi Fujiwara
Hiroshi Fujiwara is a renowned Japanese artist who has gained international acclaim for his transformative approach to upcycling. His artwork often features repurposed materials,

ranging from reclaimed wood to discarded metal objects. By meticulously transforming these waste materials into intricate sculptures and installations, Fujiwara not only creates visually stunning pieces but also sparks conversations about waste, sustainability, and the beauty that can arise from reimagining the old.

2. Business Spotlight: Patagonia's Worn Wear Program

Patagonia, the well-known outdoor clothing company, has taken strides towards reducing waste through its innovative Worn Wear program. Recognizing that many garments have a longer lifespan than what consumers typically perceive, Patagonia provides repair services for their products, extending their usefulness and ensuring that they don't end up in landfill prematurely. This initiative promotes the mindset of appreciating and caring for what we already own rather than constantly seeking new replacements - a true embodiment of Mottainai principles.

3. Artist Profile: El Anatsui

El Anatsui, a Ghanaian sculptor, has gained worldwide acclaim for his awe-inspiring tapestries made from discarded bottle caps and other found materials. His monumental artworks tell stories of cultural heritage, globalization, and environmental consciousness. Through his choice of unconventional materials and meticulous craftsmanship, Anatsui challenges our perception of waste and reminds us of the immense creative potential hidden within discarded objects.

4. Business Spotlight: The Soap Dispensary

Located in Vancouver, Canada, The Soap Dispensary is a business committed to reducing waste and promoting sustainable living through its range of refillable household and personal care products. By encouraging customers to bring their own containers and refill them, The Soap Dispensary eliminates the need for single-use plastic packaging. Their dedication to waste reduction aligns perfectly with Mottainai principles and inspires customers to be more conscious of their consumption habits.

5. Artist Profile: Haroshi

Haroshi, a Japanese skateboarder turned artist, creates stunning sculptures by repurposing discarded skateboard decks. Through his meticulous craftsmanship, he transforms broken and worn-out decks into intricate structures that capture the essence of skateboarding culture while offering a fresh perspective on waste. Haroshi's work serves as a powerful reminder that even seemingly insignificant objects can be given new life when viewed through the lens of Mottainai.

These examples highlight just a few of the countless artists and businesses that have integrated Mottainai principles into their upcycling practices. By repurposing waste materials, these individuals and organizations not only create unique and meaningful works of art but also inspire others to see the potential in what might otherwise be discarded. Their commitment to sustainability and creativity serves as an invitation for all of us to explore our own creative potential and rethink our relationship with waste.

Resources and Tips for Getting Started:

Now that you're inspired to embark on your upcycling and repurposing journey, this section will provide you with valuable resources, tools, and tips to help you get started. Whether you're a beginner or an experienced creator, these suggestions will assist you in transforming waste into works of art while keeping Mottainai principles at the forefront of your mind.

When it comes to upcycling and repurposing, one of the most critical aspects is the materials used. By choosing the right materials, you can ensure that your creations are sustainable and align with Mottainai principles. Consider working with materials such as old clothing, discarded furniture, broken ceramics, outdated electronics, and even natural elements like driftwood or fallen leaves. These materials offer endless possibilities for transformation.

In terms of tools, there are a few essentials that every upcycler should have in their toolkit. A good set of basic hand tools, including screwdrivers, pliers, and a utility knife, will prove invaluable for disassembling items and preparing materials for repurposing. Depending on your specific projects, you may also want to invest in power tools like a drill or jigsaw. Don't forget to prioritize safety by wearing protective gear such as gloves and goggles when necessary.

In addition to physical resources and tools, it's important to consider sustainability in sourcing materials for your upcycling projects. Look for local thrift stores, flea markets, or online platforms where you can find pre-loved items at affordable prices. Not only does this support the Mottainai principle of mindful consumption by giving new life to discarded objects, but it also reduces the demand for newly manufactured goods.

If you're interested in exploring more specialized techniques or learning from experienced upcyclers, consider attending workshops or classes in your community or online. These opportunities can provide valuable guidance, insights, and inspiration as you develop your skills in upcycling and repurposing. Seek out local artists, artisans, or organizations that offer workshops, demonstrations, or even mentorship programs.

Online platforms and communities dedicated to upcycling and repurposing are also great resources for learning and sharing ideas. Join forums, social media groups, and websites where you can interact with like-minded individuals, exchange tips, ask questions, and find inspiration. These platforms often feature tutorials, step-by-step guides, and challenges that can spur your creativity and help you hone your craft.

Finally, remember that upcycling and repurposing is as much about the process as it is about the end result. Embrace experimentation, playfulness, and a willingness to learn from your successes and failures. Enjoy the journey of transforming waste into unique works of art while making a positive impact on the environment.

By utilizing these resources and tips for getting started with upcycling and repurposing, you'll be well on your way to embracing Mottainai-inspired practices and creating meaningful and sustainable creations. Let your imagination run wild, and enjoy the fulfillment that comes from turning waste into beauty.

CONCLUSION

Throughout the book, we have explored the fascinating concept of Mottainai and its potential for personal and global transformation. As we conclude our journey, let us recap the key takeaways that will guide us in embracing Mottainai principles for a happier, richer, and more fulfilled life.

First and foremost, Mottainai urges us to cultivate a deep sense of regret over waste and embrace the idea of 'no waste' in all aspects of life. By adopting this mindset, we begin to see resources as precious and valuable, making conscious choices about how we utilize and consume them.

We have learned about the historical roots of Mottainai in Japan, where it has been seamlessly integrated into the cultural fabric for centuries. From beautifully upcycled garments to meticulously repurposed household items, the Japanese people have showcased their intuitive understanding of making the most out of what they possess.

Mottainai goes beyond mere conservation practices; it extends to sustainable living, environmental conservation, cultural preservation, economic efficiency, and mindful consumption habits. By incorporating Mottainai into these facets of our lives, we create profound positive changes that benefit ourselves and the planet.

Practical application is essential in fully embracing Mottainai principles. We have provided guidance on how to reduce waste in everyday life, embrace long-lasting products, develop mindfulness in consumption choices, and declutter to simplify our living spaces. These actions allow us to shift from disposable to durable, fostering a lifestyle rooted in Mottainai values.

Creating an impact requires spreading awareness about Mottainai and encouraging others to embrace its principles. Education, community engagement, and advocacy play pivotal roles in driving personal and global transformation through Mottainai. By sharing our knowledge and experiences with others, we can inspire collective action and collaboration.

Recognizing that challenges may arise along this transformative journey is crucial. We have addressed common concerns and provided strategies for overcoming obstacles. We must navigate societal pressures, maintain motivation, and continually seek new ways to integrate Mottainai into our lives and communities.

As we envision the future shaped by Mottainai principles, we understand that personal transformation is intertwined with global transformation. By embracing Mottainai, we contribute to a more sustainable, equitable, and fulfilling world. Through collective action and collaboration, we have the power to create lasting change.

Our journey from waste to wealth has unveiled the immense potential of Mottainai in transforming our lives and the world around us. Let us embrace these principles wholeheartedly, mindful of our resource utilization, grateful for what we possess, and committed to leaving a positive impact for future generations. The path forward towards personal and global transformation begins with each one of us embracing Mottainai for a happier, richer, and more fulfilled life.

Practical Application of Mottainai Principles:

Now that you have gained a deep understanding of Mottainai and its potential for personal and global transformation, it's time to put these principles into action. In this section, we will explore practical ways in which you can start embracing Mottainai in your daily life and make a tangible impact on the environment and your own well-being.

1. Reduce, Reuse, Recycle: The three R's of environmental conservation are at the core of Mottainai principles. Start by assessing your consumption habits and identifying areas where you can reduce waste. Embrace a minimalist lifestyle by prioritizing quality over quantity and resisting the temptation of impulsive purchases. Instead, focus on reusing items as much as possible. Get creative with repurposing old or unused items and think beyond traditional recycling methods.

2. Mindful Consumption: Cultivate mindfulness in your consumption choices by asking yourself important questions before making a purchase. Consider the longevity and durability of the item, its environmental impact, and whether you truly need it. Practice delayed gratification, allowing yourself time to reflect on whether the purchase aligns with your values and contributes to a more fulfilled life. By embracing mindful consumption habits, you can avoid unnecessary waste and focus on what truly brings you joy and satisfaction.

3. Embrace Sustainable Living Practices: Look for opportunities to incorporate sustainable living practices into various aspects of your life. Reduce energy consumption by using energy-efficient appliances, optimizing natural light, and minimizing reliance on fossil fuels. Adopt eco-friendly alternatives such as reusable shopping bags, water bottles, and containers. Choose plant-based or locally sourced food options to reduce your carbon footprint. Implement composting systems to divert organic waste from landfills. These small changes can have a significant positive impact on the planet.

4. Support Ethical Brands and Businesses: Use your purchasing power to support brands and businesses that align with Mottainai principles. Look for companies that prioritize sustainability,

fair labor practices, and waste reduction in their production processes. Choose products that are made from recycled materials, are designed for durability, or can be easily repaired. By supporting ethical brands, you contribute to creating a demand for sustainable products and send a message to industries that environmental consciousness is important to consumers.

5. Share Resources within Your Community: Embrace the power of community sharing by participating in local initiatives such as tool libraries, clothing swaps, or carpooling programs. By sharing resources, you not only reduce waste but also foster a sense of community and connection with those around you. Explore opportunities to lend or borrow items, share skills, or collaborate on projects. This sense of collective responsibility and resourcefulness can have a transformative impact on both individuals and communities.

6. Educate and Inspire Others: Share your knowledge and passion for Mottainai with others. Educate your family, friends, and colleagues about the concept and its potential for positive change. Organize workshops or events to teach practical skills such as upcycling or composting. Engage in conversations about the importance of reducing waste and adopting sustainable practices. By inspiring others to embrace Mottainai, you contribute to a ripple effect of change that extends far beyond your immediate circle.

Remember, embracing Mottainai is a journey, and it may require patience and persistence to fully integrate these principles into your life. Start small, celebrate progress, and be open to learning from challenges along the way. With each mindful choice you make, you contribute to personal well-being and the greater good of our planet. Together, we can create a world where waste is minimized, resources are revered, and everyone can experience a happier, richer, and more fulfilled life.

Creating an impact is a crucial aspect of embracing Mottainai for personal and global transformation. By spreading awareness about the concept and encouraging others to adopt its principles, individuals can contribute to a larger movement towards a more sustainable and mindful way of living.

One important avenue for creating an impact is through education. By incorporating Mottainai principles into educational curricula at all levels, from primary schools to universities, we can instill values of conservation, sustainability, and waste reduction in the next generation. Education plays a fundamental role in shaping attitudes and behaviors, and by teaching young people about the importance of Mottainai, we can inspire them to become agents of change.

Community engagement is another powerful tool for promoting personal and global transformation through Mottainai. Encouraging communities to come together and embrace the principles of resource sharing, waste reduction, and sustainable living can have a profound impact. This can be achieved through community events, workshops, and initiatives that foster collaboration and collective action. By creating spaces for dialogue and knowledge exchange, communities can find innovative solutions to local challenges while contributing to the larger global movement towards Mottainai.

Advocacy also plays a crucial role in driving personal and global transformation through Mottainai. Individuals can become advocates for sustainable living by actively promoting Mottainai principles within their social circles, workplaces, or even on a larger scale through social media and public speaking engagements. By sharing their own experiences, success stories, and practical tips for embracing Mottainai, advocates can inspire others to adopt these principles and multiply the positive impact.

It is important to recognize that embracing Mottainai may come with its own challenges. Overcoming societal pressures, navigating consumer culture, and addressing economic barriers are among the obstacles that individuals may face on their journey towards personal and global transformation. However, by staying committed to the principles of Mottainai and supporting one another through shared experiences and resources, individuals can overcome these challenges and continue making a difference.

Looking ahead, the vision for a future shaped by Mottainai principles is one of collective action and collaboration. It is a future where individuals, communities, and societies come together to prioritize sustainable living, mindful consumption, and waste reduction. By continuing to explore new ways to integrate Mottainai into our lives, engaging in ongoing dialogue, and fostering partnerships, we can work towards achieving widespread change and creating a world that values the preservation of resources and the well-being of both people and the planet.

In conclusion, creating an impact through spreading awareness about Mottainai and encouraging others to embrace its principles is essential for personal and global transformation. Education, community engagement, advocacy, and overcoming challenges are all key components of this journey. By envisioning a future shaped by Mottainai principles and actively working towards it, we can drive positive change and create a more sustainable, fulfilling, and harmonious world for generations to come.

Overcoming Challenges and Obstacles:
Recognizing that embracing Mottainai may come with its own set of challenges, this section offers strategies for overcoming obstacles and staying committed to the journey. It addresses common concerns specific to embracing Mottainai principles and provides tips for navigating societal pressures and maintaining motivation.

1. Addressing Skepticism: One common challenge individuals may face when embracing Mottainai is skepticism from others who may not understand or appreciate the concept. This section provides guidance on effectively communicating the benefits and importance of Mottainai, presenting evidence and examples to support one's choices, and finding common ground with skeptics.

2. Dealing with Peer Pressure: In a society where excessive consumption is often seen as the norm, individuals embracing Mottainai principles may encounter peer pressure to conform or indulge in wasteful practices. This section offers strategies for resisting the influence of peer pressure, including seeking like-minded communities and support systems, setting personal boundaries, and developing self-confidence in one's choices.

3. Overcoming Convenience Culture: Living in a world driven by convenience, it can be challenging to break free from the convenience trap and adopt more mindful consumption habits. This section provides practical tips for navigating convenience culture, such as planning ahead, prioritizing quality over convenience, and finding joy in slow living and intentional decision-making.

4. Tackling Impatience: Embracing Mottainai requires patience and a long-term perspective. This section discusses strategies for addressing impatience and staying committed to the journey, including setting realistic goals, celebrating small victories, practicing self-compassion, and focusing on the positive impacts of Mottainai choices.

5. Managing Financial Considerations: While embracing Mottainai can lead to financial savings in the long run, there may be upfront costs associated with adopting certain sustainable practices or purchasing durable products. This section offers practical advice for managing financial considerations, such as budgeting, prioritizing investments, and exploring cost-effective alternatives.

6. Navigating Social Expectations: Society often places emphasis on material possessions and status symbols, which can create pressure to accumulate and consume more. This section provides strategies for navigating social expectations, including reframing success and fulfillment, seeking alternative measures of value and achievement, and finding supportive communities that align with Mottainai principles.

7. Staying Motivated: Sustaining motivation and commitment to embracing Mottainai is crucial for long-term personal and global transformation. This section offers tips for staying motivated, such as regularly reminding oneself of the environmental and personal benefits of Mottainai, practicing self-reflection and mindfulness, engaging in self-care activities, and celebrating progress along the journey.

By addressing these common challenges and providing practical strategies for overcoming them, readers will feel empowered to navigate potential obstacles with confidence and continue their journey towards personal and global transformation through embracing Mottainai principles.

Looking Ahead

As we have learned throughout this book, embracing Mottainai is not just a personal journey, but also a collective effort towards creating positive change in the world. Looking ahead, it is essential for us to reflect on the progress we have made and envision a future where Mottainai principles are deeply ingrained in our society.

One way to continue integrating Mottainai into our lives is by exploring new avenues for sustainable living. This can involve exploring alternative energy sources, supporting local and organic agriculture, and adopting eco-friendly technologies. By staying informed about the latest advancements in sustainability and making conscious choices aligned with Mottainai principles, we can actively contribute to a greener future.

Another important aspect of looking ahead is fostering a sense of community and collaboration. By engaging with our neighbors, friends, and colleagues, we can create networks of like-minded individuals who share a common passion for Mottainai. Together, we can organize events, workshops, and initiatives that promote waste reduction, resource sharing, and mindful consumption. By working together, we amplify the impact of our individual actions and inspire others to join the movement.

Additionally, embracing Mottainai on a larger scale requires advocacy and education. We must spread awareness about the importance of Mottainai principles and their potential for personal and global transformation. This can be done through workshops, public speaking engagements, and social media campaigns. By sharing our own experiences and knowledge, we can inspire others to adopt Mottainai practices and become agents of change in their own communities.

While embracing Mottainai may come with its own set of challenges, it is crucial for us to stay committed to the journey. Recognize that change takes time and that setbacks are a natural part of any transformative process. Surround yourself with a supportive network of individuals who share your values and can provide encouragement when needed. Seek inspiration from the success stories of individuals and businesses who have embraced Mottainai, reminding yourself of the positive impact you can make by staying true to these principles.

In conclusion, looking ahead means envisioning a future where Mottainai principles are deeply embedded in every aspect of our lives. It requires us to explore new ways to integrate Mottainai, engage with our communities, advocate for change, and stay committed to the journey despite obstacles. By continuing on this path, we contribute to a more sustainable, harmonious world, where waste is minimized, resources are valued, and fulfillment is derived from living in harmony with nature and each other. Embrace Mottainai as a powerful tool for personal and global transformation, and let us create a better world together.

Printed in Poland
by Amazon Fulfillment
Poland Sp. z o.o., Wrocław

33082355R00072